D1548678

DATE DUE

THE COMMONWEALTH AND INTERNATIONAL LIBRARY
Joint Chairmen of the Honorary Editorial Advisory Board
SIR ROBERT ROBINSON, O.M., F.R.S., LONDON
DEAN ATHELSTAN SPILHAUS, MINNESOTA
Publisher: ROBERT MAXWELL, M.C., M.P.

THE ESSENTIALS OF MARKETING SERIES
General Editors: BERNARD TAYLOR AND D. W. SMALLBONE

Marketing and Financial Control

Marketing and Financial Control

BY

A. S. JOHNSON

PERGAMON PRESS

OXFORD · LONDON · EDINBURGH · NEW YORK

TORONTO · SYDNEY · PARIS · BRAUNSCHWEIG

PERGAMON PRESS LTD.,
Headington Hill Hall, Oxford
4 & 5 Fitzroy Square, London W.1

PERGAMON PRESS (SCOTLAND) LTD.,
2 & 3 Teviot Place, Edinburgh 1

PERGAMON PRESS INC.,
44–01 21st Street, Long Island City, New York 11101

PERGAMON OF CANADA, LTD.,
6 Adelaide Street East, Toronto, Ontario

PERGAMON PRESS (AUST.) PTY. LTD.,
Rushcutters Bay, Sydney, New South Wales

PERGAMON PRESS S.A.R.L.,
24 rue des Écoles, Paris 5^e

VIEWEG & SOHN GMBH,
Burgplatz 1, Braunschweig

Printed in Great Britain by A. Wheaton & Co., Exeter and London

TO JEANNE

Contents

Editors' Foreword to Series

THIS is a series of practical marketing handbooks written by British experts and designed as a library providing a compact and comprehensive review of modern marketing practice and technique.

The books are intended for sales and marketing managers, for marketing trainees and students of management, and for businessmen and managers of all kinds who are looking for an up-to-date, concise, readable statement of how the best British companies market their products.

Marketing as an accepted part of a business enterprise is a phenomenon of the last 10 years. Until then companies made goods and hoped that, by good fortune or through sales pressure, customers would be persuaded to buy them. As business has become more competitive, first in the consumer market and increasingly also in industrial markets, British managements have begun to appreciate the need for a rigorous and systematic approach to the market.

So much of the marketing approach seems obvious; it is surprising that the development of marketing thought and techniques should have spread so slowly through British industry. However, it is now possible to make a critical review of the best marketing practices in British industry. It is thus the purpose of this series to provide in simple terms descriptions and case studies demonstrating established techniques which can be used by the modern marketing executive to build for his company a strong position in the market and so make an important contribution to his company's profitability and contribute to the overall good of the community by ensuring that more and more people will be able to buy what they genuinely want and fewer customers will have to put up with second best.

The series has been so organized that, while each volume is self-contained, a connective thread runs through each so that the whole series will provide a compact and comprehensive review of marketing practice and techniques.

The editors would welcome at any time comments and criticism from their readers, and particularly suggestions for further additions to the range. The following titles are either available now or are in preparation:

Marketing Overseas
Marketing and the Brand Manager
Marketing through Research
Marketing and Financial Control
Marketing and the Computer

BERNARD TAYLOR
D. W. SMALLBONE

Editor's Foreword

UNTIL recently the value of the accountant in marketing has been suspect. He has been looked upon either with suspicion or doubt as someone who only considered figures when marketing men were convinced that people were more important. At best he was a recorder of history; at worst a positive barrier to progress.

Whether this was ever true is doubtful, it is certainly not true today.

Proper marketing planning will always envisage alternative situations and in the final analysis the selection of the "right" decision will be determined by the financial outcome of profit in terms of volume or capital employed or some other convenient financial comparison.

The ability to cost accurately both in terms of past experience and future expectation, taking into account the hazards of the economic system, is the province of the management accountant.

In simple and understandable terms, this book sets out to describe this rôle. It is hoped that it will do much to dispel the still existing suspicion of accountants by marketing men and demonstrate that the kind of support that they can give is invaluable to any organization that puts a premium on marketing efficiency. It is hoped also that many accountants will be stimulated to make a positive contribution to marketing by a better understanding of the marketing man's financial needs.

Ashridge Management College   D. W. SMALLBONE
April 1967

Author's Preface

THIS book has been written for marketing people who have little or no knowledge of business finance. It describes the financial dimensions and implications of business activity, and stresses the rôle of the marketing function in securing financial success. My assumption in writing this book has been that an understanding of basic business finance and accounts will help marketing people to contribute more effectively to the growth and prosperity of the organizations and the economy they serve.

Finance is not everyone's favourite subject, so I have tried to unfold the story in an interesting way which will encourage the reader to persevere. Throughout the book I have used illustrations drawn from familiar marketing situations. I hope this will help the reader to develop the additional confidence which a grasp of sound financial principles can give to anyone who works in a business organization.

The book does not offer any novel techniques. We have techniques in plenty, and our business problems stem more from not using the techniques we have than from not having the techniques to use. This book is offered in the hope that it will enable marketing people to understand, adapt, and apply financial techniques to their own marketing problems. This should lead to better decisions and performance and to more fruitful relationships between the marketing and accounting functions. If it achieves this, the book will be a worth-while contribution to the integration of functional specialisms so essential in business today.

I gratefully acknowledge help from many quarters. In particular I should like to thank Mr. A. P. Robson, also of Ashridge Management College, for the many illuminating discussions we have had on accounting topics. He will recognize his own enthusiasm for business finance and management accounting in these pages. I must also thank Mr. D. W. Smallbone, the general editor of this series, for his original invitation to write this book and his continued interest ever since.

CHAPTER 1

Marketing, Finance, and Control

HERE is a marketing situation. It is fictitious and lighthearted, but it will get us thinking about marketing, finance and control.

The End Product*

"No doubt you are wondering," said the marketing director, "why I have called this National Sales Conference. It must be pretty important, you are probably thinking, to justify bringing together the company's representatives from every hole and corner. And you would be right, gentlemen. The purpose of this conference is of unparalleled importance and the result of it will be of far-reaching consequence. In short, gentlemen, it is to introduce to you a sensational new product which has been christened with the irresistible brand-name 'Pupgrub'.

"Was that you Jenkins whom I overheard to remark 'another perishing dog-food'? If it was I'm afraid we shall have to let you go. There is no room in this dynamic and pulsating organization for anybody who is not a company-man with a characteristic company-outlook and an unmistakable company-personality. This, Jenkins, is not 'another dog-food', it is '*the* dog-food'.

"After years of complicated and painstaking research by our chemists, locked away in the laboratory, we have evolved an entirely new and exciting formula, positively crawling with protein and vitamin. 'Ah!' you may ask—though it would be somewhat imprudent to do so—'but is there a market for it?' Gentlemen, this company's marketing strategy is always based upon scientifically ascertained fact and not irresponsible assumption. I have before me a report by that eminent firm of market research consultants, Chance, Hazard & Sermize Partners, who have

---

* With acknowledgements to Dennis Ellam, F.C.A., Secretary, the National Federation of Wholesale Grocers and Provision Merchants. (Reproduced by permission.)

carefully surveyed a specially selected cross-section of young housewives. And what did they find? That 37·42 per cent of all families with a child under four who prefers porridge to breakfast cereal also have a dog. That 21·4 per cent recurring of families with a convertible 20 in. screen television set have a dog. That, among families with an 18 in. screen, the percentage soars to no less than 24·29 per cent. And, finally, you will be interested to know that one out of every three packets of dog-food in the larder is there as the result of impulse buying. I take it, gentlemen, that you know what impulse buying is—it means that, faced with a packet of 'Pupgrub', the housewife becomes prey to an irresistible surge of emotion which deprives her of will-power and self-control. She reacts as in an hypnotic trance. Reflect upon the relationship between the Monk Rasputin and the late Czarina Alexandrine of Russia, gentlemen, and you will have a rough historical parallel.

"Gentlemen, the facts speak for themselves. I have no more to say except those three little words that have so often, in the history of mankind, preceded an exciting adventure—'Go to it'."

*   *   *   *

"Three months ago, gentlemen," said the marketing director, "you left this room to embark upon a challenging enterprise. Did I say challenging? Nay!—for there can be no challenge to 'Pupgrub'. It is unique. It is the superlative. Yet the result of your combined efforts would shame a sales-force selling refrigerators to Eskimos or hair restorer to Hottentots. Our sales to date—pardon me if my voice trembles—are 1·4 per cent of budget. We have stocks to the rafters, stocks in the aisles, stocks in the factory in ever-growing piles.

"But Management in this company, faced with adversity, is never quick to lay the blame elsewhere—is ever ready to subject itself to a penetrating inward scrutiny. This we have done. And what did the penetrating inward scrutiny reveal, gentlemen? That Management was absolutely right. Chance, Hazard & Sermize Partners have made a further consumer survey—they have experimented with the housewives of Cheltenham—and what a revelation it was! Nine out of every ten semi-detached householders in Cheltenham who have a kennel also have a dog. Yet what is the size of our slice of this vast dog-food cake? Slice did I say? Ha! Ha! Gentlemen, slice forsooth!—it is hardly a sliver!—barely a crumb! And why, gentlemen?—that is what the Board wishes to know. Management deserves an explanation. Who will give Management what it deserves? Who will speak for you gormless lot?

"Ah! Jenkins—you appear to be still with us—and if I mistake not, your right arm is raised. There can be no room for doubt, my dear fellow, that one with your exceptional ability, your aged-in-the-wood judgement, your unfailing prescience, your vivid imagination, your phenomenal clarity of thought and expression can draw aside the veil past which we cannot see, can unlock the door to which we find no key. It is true, of course, that we have at your disposal production experts without equal; packaging personnel to whom presentation is a dedication;

market research surveyors whose fame is international. But it is you, Jenkins, whom Providence has draped with the mantle of omniscience—you, Jenkins, whom we are all agog to hear explain why 'Pupgrub' has not swept the country like a raging epidemic. We are waiting, Jenkins, for you to tell us the reason.''

"Well, Sir," said Jenkins, tremulously, "dogs don't like the blooming stuff."

From this rather amusing caricature of business life, we can extract and examine the three concepts which are the subject of this book: marketing, finance, and control.

Marketing

The Pupgrub story is the story of a marketing failure. Despite intense efforts to analyse demand, manufacture a product, create a brand image, assemble, organize, and motivate a field sales force and launch a sales campaign, the company can find no adequate outlet for its product. The stocks are piling up at the end of the production line. Hardly anyone is buying Pupgrub.

Now it is the nature of marketing, and of business generally, to secure customer satisfaction. (Other books in this series will explain at length how marketing does this; here we shall pick out some of the main points to show how they link with finance and control.) As we saw, there are very few customers for Pupgrub. Sales are only $1 \cdot 4\%$ of budget. We can assume that the $1 \cdot 4\%$ are not very satisfied either. The word is just not getting around that Pupgrub is the stuff to give your dog. So the company's marketing efforts, which ultimately coincide with its business efforts, are in vain.

What were these efforts? Marketing is a process or a system, a series of related activities and events each one leading to the next, and all intended to lead to customer satisfaction. There seems fairly wide agreement on the main business activities needed to give customer satisfaction, and the following list covers the main ones:

Defining the market, and the intended market share.
Developing ideas on which products or services to sell.

Finding out what competitors are doing.
Deciding on packaging and distribution methods.
Securing the availability of products.
Fixing prices.
Getting orders.
Delivering products to customers.
Securing future business.

Figure 1 converts this list into the systems framework which is a useful one for analysing business situations, and in which the basic "inputs" are always information, materials, and energy.

Defining the market and the intended market share comes high on the list of business objectives. Drucker's formulation of the objectives of a business is still widely quoted,* and he put market standing first. It is incredible how few managers in the United Kingdom possess a clear statement of the marketing objectives of the firm they work for. Yet marketing objectives—developed, clarified, and quantified year by year—are the basic milestones which, beyond all others, encourage survival, health, and growth for individual firms and whole economies. If the people running a business enterprise fail to formulate and communicate marketing objectives to executive and operating staffs, the detailed policies and instructions issued from the top will lack coherence and conviction. Yet marketing objectives are simple to express. Let's give the marketing director of the Pupgrub firm a chance to show us how, inventing some statistics for the purpose of illustration.

"Last year, the dogs of Britain ate 50,000,000 tins of manufactured dog food. Consumption is expected to rise by 4% annually over the next 5 years. At present, six main suppliers share 85% of the market. Two years from now we aim to have 25% of this expanding market." Precise quantification of objectives is not easy, but provided the percentage tolerance is known and accepted, the figures finally chosen are surely much better than none at all.

Once we have an aim, the rest follows. The next item on our list

* Drucker, P. F., *The Practice of Management*, Heinemann, London, 1955.

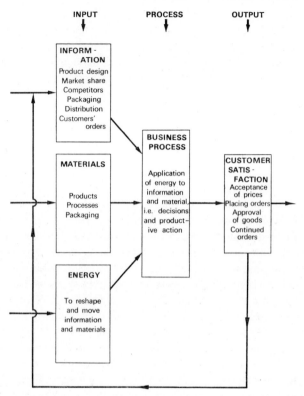

Fig. 1. Systems framework for the marketing process.

of marketing activities was to do with ideas. We have to conceive a product which will give customer satisfaction. We can start by thinking of the intrinsic nature of the product. Will it do what the customer wants it to do? Pupgrub Ltd. has a chance here to visualize its proposed product in the possession of the customer, or rather the customer's dog. What do dogs like? What mixture of protein, vitamin, and carbohydrate, with or without additives, will cause a dog to lick the plate clean in seconds, show signs of bouncing vitality, and refuse all other dog foods? Can the bio-chemists, veterinary surgeons, dog breeders and dog fanciers help us here, not to mention the dogs themselves? Research on these lines could, indeed, bring Pupgrub Ltd. to a new and exciting formula, but to a formula based on the dog's impulses rather than the impulses of its owner. For if the dog refuses to eat, the owner will surely refuse to buy.

However, the intrinsic excellence of the product is not enough in itself. It must also seem to prospective buyers to have a greater degree of intrinsic excellence than alternative, competing products. This is why the marketing process next involves having a look at what others in the same field are doing. The marketing man scrutinizes competing products because he wants to place himself in his customer's shoes at the moment of decision. It is obvious that the marketing director of Pupgrub Ltd. has no time for theorists who imagine that customers, particularly consumers of household products, carefully weigh the merits of different brands. He relies on the impulsiveness of the retail shopper who reacts as in a hypnotic trance. But is this always the case? What will the disappointed Pupgrub purchaser do next time? She will survey the shelves of dog food and say, "No, not Pupgrub. Let's try another one . . .", and there she is, weighing the alternatives again. So firms will keep an eye on competitors, their packaging, their products and their prices, as well as on their general growth or decline. The presence of competitors is always a challenge to do better, to produce and sell something different; in a word, to set objectives for innovation.

Packaging and distribution were next on the list. Packaging is important because it can offer safety on the journey and eye-appeal on the shelf. Let us hope that the post mortem which surely followed the Pupgrub story did not reveal that Pupgrub appeared before the shopper's eye in rusty or buckled tins. What-ever handling it got between the warehouse and the shop was the result of a distribution policy or lack of it. A choice between different channels of distribution should have been made, and the alternatives costed before Pupgrub Ltd. could be sure that its product would take its place in the market at the right time, in sufficient quantities, and in tip-top, eye-catching condition.

By now, you must have noticed how, in working down our list on p. 3, we are working backwards from the satisfaction of a customer to the internal activities of the firm. Within the firm, everyone either contributes to customer satisfaction or detracts from it, and it is only by planning backwards that one can maintain the relationship between what goes on in the firm and the customer satisfaction which alone can allow the internal activity to continue. On our list, the next topic was securing the availability of products. This rather wide phrase covers both purchasing (for resale) and manufacturing. We shall refer quite a bit to manufacturing in this book, not only because all selling effort is backed up by a production process somewhere down the line, but also because manufacture is an integral part of the process whereby Britain satisfies its customers; if Britain survives in world business, it will be as manufacturer rather than as middle man.

With customer satisfaction firmly in mind, our sights set on a defined market and market share, and with a blue print of the product in front of us, we can begin to plan the manufacturing processes necessary to make the product available to customers. The Pupgrub firm has a factory. Presumably it has refrigerated stores for raw meat and other ingredients, mincing, mixing and heat-processing machinery, production lines filling and sealing the cans, labelling and packaging plant, a warehouse, and offices and other useful departments. But of all these we hear nothing. The marketing director does not mention the factory until he has to report that it is piled high with stocks that are not being sold. It takes little imagination to realize that the machinery has stopped, the manufacturing skills are unwanted, the work-force is probably redundant, and the suppliers of raw ingredients are themselves not getting orders from Pupgrub. The process of manufacture is part of the process of marketing, and cannot continue unless it is leading towards customer satisfaction. If the marketing outlets fail to open, sooner or later the whole process halts and the factory gathers rust. With more attention to the security of his outlets, the marketing director of Pupgrub could have helped his production colleagues to remain productive members of the business community.

It has been said that the purpose of being in business is to submit invoices. If lorry loads of Pupgrub were rolling through the factory gates, there would be a girl in the dispatch office typing and mailing invoices. This raises the question of pricing because an invoice is a priced statement of goods delivered or services rendered, and before Pupgrub can get orders or submit invoices, the marketing director must decide or advise what the price will be. This brings us for the first time to finance and accounting.

Traditionally, the accountant helps the pricing decision by quoting manufacturing and selling costs. But this is never enough. The marketing people must find out all they can about customer reaction to different price levels, and how these reactions affect the customer's decision to buy or not to buy. In the long term, total sales revenue must cover total costs, but prices must also maintain a sales level against competition and yield a satisfactory profit as well. Pricing policies seek to reconcile these conflicting needs. The pricing decision is a complex one, and mistakes can be difficult to rectify. Nevertheless, the Pupgrub salesmen must be armed with a price-list before they can "go to it".

The salesmen set out in the hope of getting orders. The order-getting process is perhaps the activity for which field salesmen are best known. But it is clear that the actual buying/selling interview is but a tiny part of the whole process of marketing. Training in persuasion, politeness, visual aids, and so on, as a means of maximizing the effectiveness of the salesman/buyer encounter is of value, but no amount of sales training on these lines can make up for the deficiencies of mistaken demand, poor quality products, misjudging the strength of competitors, and so on—as the Pupgrub salesmen soon found out.

Ideally, the marketing man works towards a situation in which the market yields orders like ripe plums dropping from a well-laden tree. Orders, like the fruits of the earth, need long-term cultivation. Consumer and industrial needs have to be forecast and analysed, changes in demand predicted, goods and services made ready, and the attention of buyers drawn to the goods on offer. All this and more is involved in the process of marketing. Skimping the earlier stages of this process—market research, product design, advertising, and so on—will result in a dearth of orders just as surely as skimping soil preparation and pruning will result in a dearth of fruit. In the end, of course, the fruit must be plucked; orders must be clinched. Salesmen know that collecting orders calls for skills of its own. The Pupgrub salesmen, going out to the "fruit-plucking" with high hopes of applying their skills effectively, must have been keenly frustrated to find there was no fruit to pick, no demand for their product to satisfy.

Once the orders are secured, once the decision to place an order has been put on record, the marketing cycle is almost complete. (It is interesting to note in passing that the most important decisions affecting the survival and growth of a commercial organization are made outside the firm, by those who decide whether or not to buy its products. Perhaps managers ought to pay more attention to decision-getting than to decision-making.) It still remains to deliver the goods, and here the marketing people, aiming as always at customer satisfaction, are in the hands of those who physically handle the product, i.e. production, warehousing, and distribution staff. Customer satisfaction in this final phase is not, however, entirely up to the production and distribution people; they will indeed try to fulfil delivery promises, but these promises were made by sales staff who might conceivably make wild promises in an attempt to land orders. The final stages of the process call for close co-operation between producers, salesmen, and distributors. Any hitch at this stage could well jeopardize future orders.

A firm which has delivered the goods once, wants to go on doing so. A business is always assumed to be a going concern and needs a continuous supply of new orders to keep it in being. Buyers, a salesman tells himself hopefully, are creatures of habit, and will go on buying from a satisfactory source if there is no strong indication to the contrary. The supplying firm will therefore keep the quality of its products, its rate of delivery, and its prices at a level satisfactory to its customers in order to keep them on its books. And, of course, it will look for new markets for old products, and new products for old markets. Company growth and economic prosperity has no source other than this—a secure stake in the markets of the business community. This is just what Pupgrub lacks at the moment. But the company is not necessarily doomed. Perhaps it can start again where we started on p. 5, conceiving a product which will give customer satisfaction. But it can only move from failure to success if it has enough money to see it through, and this leads us to the financial dimension.

Finance

Business activities can be measured in terms of money, the universal language of economic exchange. The flow of goods from seller to buyer is matched by a return flow of money value, without which economic exchange would nowadays be impossible. Figure 2 illustrates how the financial system adds a money measure to the marketing system at Fig. 1.

The important business facts recorded in money terms by the accountant include the amount and sources of the money put down to start the business, the way in which this original investment changes into the property and materials needed to run a business, the value of sales generated by the investment, the cost of achieving those sales, the resulting profit, and the growth of the original investment. All these facts, summarized in money terms, are contained in the official annual accounts of the company which consist of the balance sheet (or statement of financial position) and the profit and loss account (or income statement). These statements, to be explained in more detail in succeeding chapters, show the financial results of marketing operations. To illustrate the financial implications of trying to capture a market, we can turn again to the attempts to market Pupgrub.

The first four stages, defining the market to deciding on packaging and distribution, do not necessarily cost very much money.

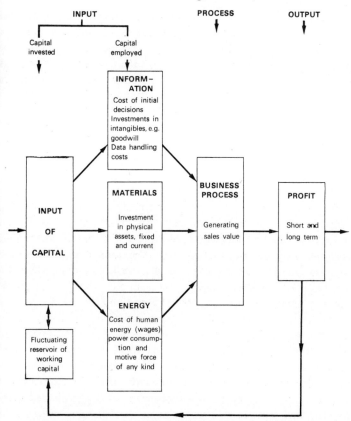

Fig. 2. Financial dimensions of a marketing process involving
manufacture.

One can, indeed, spend a fair amount on market research, packaging consultants, and inter-firm comparisons, but these first four items are largely concerned with ideas, and money cannot in itself call forth ideas. Before a man can start up a business, or think of applying money to a business venture, he must already be sure of which market he is in, how much of it he intends to make his own, what products he will offer, whether he will make or buy, and so on. Until he has made up his mind on these points, he is in no position to persuade an investor to put money into the business or to begin spending the money if the original capital is his own. A going concern will spend money on the four things that head our list only if it is large enough to employ or consult with market intelligence specialists or run a research and development section.

Pupgrub Ltd. probably spent little in this direction. But it certainly owned or rented a factory, installed plant and equipment, bought raw materials and hired operators, clerks, and managers to run the place. This took a lot of money, and the accountant of Pupgrub Ltd. recorded in his books what it cost to do these things. Day by day he accumulated the costs of putting raw ingredients through the process; day by day he transferred work-in-progress costs to a finished goods account. All he now required was to transfer the cost of finished goods through a cost of goods sold account to a profit and loss account, there to be matched with the corresponding sales value of goods delivered. But, as we know, he had little work to do on these latter accounts. The finished goods account grew in value as crates of Pupgrub reached the rafters. And as the total of finished stock increased, so did the total of cash on hand and at bank diminish. Sales or no sales, the operators, clerks, and managers wanted their pay, and the suppliers wanted their money. So did the salesmen, whose quest for orders bore so little fruit. The firm would cheerfully have met delivery costs, had any been incurred. Faced with the failure of Pupgrub, the only way for the firm to survive was to inves its remaining cash, if any, in new ideas for a product which would sell and satisfy.

In the period covered by the Pupgrub story, the accountant would be bound to report an enormous loss. Although a company normally regards its finished stocks as an asset, awaiting only a customer's willingness to buy before being turned into a profitable sale, Pupgrub Ltd. would have to face the fact that its finished stocks were unsaleable. Stocks are traditionally valued at the lower of cost or market value. The cost of the finished Pupgrub was very high, but the market value was nil. The cost of all the stocks would therefore be written off against the sales revenue for the period.

And the sales revenue was only 1·4% of budget—hence there would be a loss.

Profits retained in a business remain the property of the owners of the business and therefore increase the original investment of the owners. Likewise, losses have to be borne by the owners, and reduce the original investment. The question with Pupgrub is, can the remaining investment support a programme of successful redevelopment? Is there sufficient cash to keep the company going while new products are conceived, new markets sought? Or does the company need more cash to give it breathing space for development? How hard are creditors pressing? Will the bank give an overdraft?

The rest of this book will attempt to explain in more detail how and why accountants record and report on the financial aspect of business events. Their basic purpose in doing this is to provide the people who own and operate the business with information on the changing state of the business as it operates in its environment. Information of this kind is intended to help in the control of the business, and this leads in to our third major concept.

Control

Dictionaries define "control" in many ways: "to check or verify, and hence to regulate; to call to account, reprove; to exercise restraint or direction upon the free action of". These are some of the definitions offered by the *Shorter OED*. Webster gets nearer to the business situation with: "to check, test or verify by counter or parallel evidence; verify by comparison or research."

Control systems in business are receiving widespread attention these days; mathematicians, behavioural scientists, accountants, engineers, and others are all concerned with the attempt to explain and improve control. The simplest description of control is, perhaps, that it is the process which brings about intended or desirable conditions. First, it is a process, a series of interrelated events, a system; then, it brings something about, i.e. it exercises a positive influence on events, not leaving things to chance or hope; it seeks to bring about a set of definable, recognizable conditions which confer some advantage or benefit not at present possessed, and which are preferable to present conditions; these preferable conditions are therefore desirable, and the controller controls with the intention of bringing them about. The basic events or factors in a control system can therefore be summarized like this:

> Knowledge of an objective to be reached.
> Knowledge of progress made.
> Comparison of objectives and progress.
> Corrective action if progress towards objectives is unsatisfactory.

Figure 3 illustrates the elements of a control system. It shows how control systems extend operating systems and keep activities or operations moving towards objectives (the desired conditions) by a circular and continuous process. The output or results of the operating system are measured and compared with the desired output or results. This comparison often reveals a discrepancy between actual and desired results. Up to this point, the control process consists of a flow of information, the communication of messages about the operating process. If the messages reveal a discrepancy (i.e. a description of the extent to which the desired conditions are not being reached), there is an undesirable condition, a condition to be avoided. Awareness of the discrepancy therefore stimulates a renewed input of energy intended to put an end to the discrepancy itself, and so make actual results coincide with desired results. In familiar terms, this is "taking corrective action".

The threefold notion of aims, progress, and correction are all-pervasive in the natural order, and are certainly at the root of business success. The whole of the Pupgrub story is shot through with examples of it.

"No doubt you are wondering why I have called this conference", began the marketing director. The salesmen are uncertain about the aim of the conference and are powerless to make progress until they know what the aim is. An absence of aim may

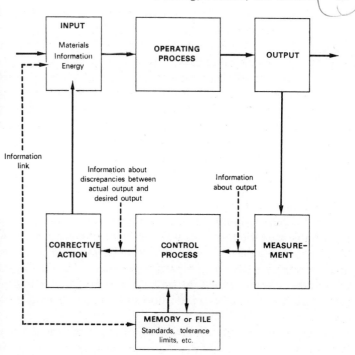

Fig. 3. Operating system with control loop.

initially be intriguing, but if prolonged is either paralysing or liberating, depending on how much one is in need of an aim at that particular moment.

The aim turns out to be the introduction of Pupgrub. Immediately we get an example of conflicting aims. Jenkins does not wish to sell dog food. He aims to make his mark as a salesman of other products. His acute disappointment with the objective of the conference produces in him a state of tension and frustration. This physical condition is undesirable and demands relief or correction. His corrective action, possibly involuntary, is to mutter "Another perishing dog food".

At this point the marketing director gets some measure of the results he is achieving in attempting to stir up enthusiasm for Pupgrub. In systems jargon, he gets some "feedback". The feedback is in fact Jenkins' remark, "Another perishing dog food", and this gives the marketing director the message that he is not succeeding. There is a discrepancy between what he wants to achieve and what he is actually achieving. Awareness of this discrepancy stimulates the marketing director to put forth energy to remove it. So he threatens Jenkins with the sack. Does this help the marketing director to achieve his aim, i.e. to make Jenkins feel enthusiastic about Pupgrub? Almost certainly not; all it does is to terminate the discrepancy messages, which means in effect destroying the control system.

As far as Jenkins himself is concerned, he is given a vision of the undesirable condition towards which *sotto voce* remarks will lead him. To maintain the desirable condition of having a job, he makes no more remarks. His search for alternative ways of dissipating his frustration is not described for us, but we can be sure he finds it absorbing, and that he hears little more of the marketing director's speech.

So far we have detected more avoidance of undesirable situations than active pursuit of desirable ones. It is hardly surprising that the venture comes to grief. Nevertheless, the marketing director tries to be positive. He announces that the Pupgrub chemists have achieved their objective (which was product innovation) and assures his sales force that prospective buyers will desire to possess new-formula Pupgrub if only their attention is drawn to it. The marketing director wishes the firm to move from its present situation (Pupgrub stocks but no orders) to a more desirable situation (Pupgrub stocks with customers placing orders). Beyond that there are yet more desirable situations: satisfied customers, invoices flowing outwards, cash flowing back in, profit accumulating; all this the company hopes for, and looks to its control system to report actual events which will coincide with hopes.

The control system, however, sends messages which reveal alarming discrepancies between actual and desired results. Stock levels are way beyond what is necessary in a manufacturing company, and sales are only $1 \cdot 4\%$ of budget. The need for corrective action is pressing, but the company is unsure of how to reapply energy to its operating system. The control process is extended by convening another sales conference, the aim of this second conference being to find out which part of the operating system is failing. It cannot, for example, be a failure of market research; a second survey confirms the earlier one. Let the salesmen themselves explain why they are failing to achieve what they set out to achieve, i.e. to get orders. We saw that control systems begin with an input of information, and so the key man at this crucial control stage is the man with most information. It turns out to be the omniscient Jenkins. The information that he brings—the feedback —is accurate and compelling: "Dogs don't like the blooming stuff."

But the information comes too late. The "production experts without equal" have by now produced unwanted Pupgrub in large quantities. It is useless now for the marketing director to use up control energy in exhorting his sales force to do better. Nor should he waste it pleading with the dogs. His original objective, to sell Pupgrub in budgeted quantities, is unattainable, and the energy generated by the control system should be absorbed in the search for other—attainable—objectives. In this case, it means going back to the beginning of the marketing process and making a fresh start. The corrective action will then be applied to stage one of the marketing process with a better prospect of success at subsequent stages. Granted a sufficient reservoir of working capital, the whole operating and control process will start again.

From these not too serious examples, we can draw some general ideas about the control process, particularly as it applies to a group of people working in a business:

1. A shared perception of a desirable situation (i.e. an objective) seems to be the best means of getting people to work together in trying to bring about that situation.
2. In the business context these "desirable situations" take the

form of objectives, standards, tolerance limits, budgets, and so on.

3. People will continue to work towards objectives if they know how well they are doing, i.e. what progress they are making.
4. Strong feedback carrying messages of failure will tempt the recipient to attack the control system rather than take corrective action.*
5. Progress information is needed most of all by the person who will actually take corrective action (should this be necessary) rather than by intermediaries in the chain of communication.
6. Progress information should come neither too late (when resources are irreversibly committed) nor too early (before genuine trends are discernible).
7. When feedback shows that objectives are unattainable, the corrective action takes the form of a search for alternative objectives which are attainable.
8. There is never an absence of objectives; if business leaders fail to establish and communicate objectives, others in the business will frame their own objectives, usually achieving less for the business by having to do so.

The process of control, then, consists in describing desirable situations and the activities which lead to their achievement. The financial situation of a business is described in its balance sheets, which can indicate more or less desirable financial conditions existing at different points of time. The activities leading to the balance-sheet situation can be expressed in financial terms and summarized in the profit and loss account or income statement; these activities, and the corresponding profit and loss account, will cover a period of time. The next two chapters will explain these accounting documents more fully.

---

* In classical tragedy the messenger who brings bad news is often in danger of his life. This accounts for the "good news" complex which dominating businessmen tend to engender in their subordinates, thus distorting their own perception of the situation and possibly piling up trouble for themselves later on.

Summary

The process of marketing is coterminous with the whole cycle of business, beginning with decisions on which markets to enter and what products to offer, and leading on through purchasing and production, order-getting, and delivery to a final exchange which encourages a continuing relationship between buyer and seller, a relationship which brings satisfaction to the customer and profit to the selling company.

Events in this process have a financial equivalent which needs to be planned and controlled. Money will flow into the business and be put to use in securing goods and services for resale. Trading brings back into the business sufficient money to pay for the cost of operations and leave a profit. The money measure is the only universal measure of trading ability and economic growth, and takes pride of place among the information systems which provide business control.

The control process describes present situations and contrasts them with future, more desirable, situations which it is intended to reach. It then compares information on aims with knowledge of progress to date in pursuing these aims, highlights discrepancies between aims and progress, and takes corrective action. In financial terms, situations are reported in balance sheets. The financial results of progress during a period of time are reported in profit and loss accounts.

B

CHAPTER 2

A Financial Base
for Marketing Operations

MARKETING operations, which usually involve financial risk, need the support of a sound financial position. The financial position, or condition, of a business is reflected to the outside world in an annual statement called a balance sheet. This chapter will explain the way in which balance sheets summarize the financial condition which acts as a base from which marketing effort is launched.

A balance sheet describes the financial position of a company rather more carefully than a private individual would describe his financial position. Most individuals would just count up how much money they had. But a businessman would draw up two lists. The first list would show what the business owned at a certain date, and the second list would show where finance was raised to support the purchase or ownership of the things owned. The things owned list he would head "assets" (which would normally include many things other than cash) and the second list would be called "sources". Side by side, these two lists would form a balance sheet.

There are two basic notions about a balance sheet: firstly, that it always balances (total sources must equal total assets) and, secondly, that it describes the position at one point of time only.

As Fig. 3 shows, the money invested in a business is turned into assets. All the finance in a business is turned into all the assets, which is why the two sides of a balance sheet must always balance.

The simplest balance sheet is the balance sheet of a business which has just started up. A young man called Antonio has just gone into business with a new ice-cream recipe which he hopes

ill be popular with the Margate trippers. He has saved up £100
of capital with which to start. His first balance sheet is as shown
n Table 1.

TABLE 1. ANTONIO'S ICE-CREAM

Balance Sheet as at 1 May 19.. (10 a.m.)

Sources	Assets
Capital £100	Cash £100

Antonio has the money in a tin under his bed. But he wants to
open a bank account. If, on his way to the bank, he loses a £5
note, both sides of the balance sheet are affected. His cash, now
banked, is £95, and likewise his capital is now only £95. If, how-
ver, he had spent the £5 on ingredients, the balance sheet would
have changed in a different way (Table 2).

TABLE 2. ANTONIO'S ICE-CREAM

Balance Sheet at at 1 May 19.. (10.30 a.m.)

Sources	£	Assets	£
Capital	100	Stock (of ingredients)	5
		Cash	95
	£100		£100

The purchase of ingredients merely changes the form in which the
assets are held (£5 of cash changes into £5's worth of ingredients).
Antonio's capital remains at £100, and the balance sheet still
balances.

It is obvious that the financial position of a business is always
changing. To measure and report on it, accountants have to take
a point of time and relate all source and asset values to that point
of time. To do otherwise would create a picture so distorted as to
be meaningless. Thus, a balance sheet is like a still photograph
taken from a movie reel. In itself, it tells us nothing about what
sources or assets are changing or how fast the rate of change. It
merely states how sources balanced with assets at this particular

moment of time. For this reason company accounts always show
the previous year's balance-sheet figures alongside the newly
reported figures, thus revealing the changes in financial structure
that have occurred between the two balance-sheet dates.

To understand these changes, we must first understand the
structure of a balance sheet in some detail. The explanation which
follows will describe the items commonly found in balance sheets
and will then discuss how the accountant puts a money value to
these items. In Chapter 4 we shall look at some balance-sheet
ratios which we can use to get an idea of financial strength or
weakness. All the time we shall bear in mind the relevance of these
concepts to the marketing man.

Balance-sheet Items

The assets owned by a business are its cash and the useful things
it buys to support marketing operations. Assets fall into categories
representing the familiar things most businesses need, and we can
see these categories develop as we watch Antonio start business
operations. After buying his ingredients and banking the rest of his
money, Antonio goes on to buy a barrow and mixing and freezing
equipment. The barrow comes from a friend, who takes a cheque
for £2 for it. The mixing and freezing equipment comes to £80,
also paid for by cheque. This is a lot of money, but Antonio thinks
they will last him at least 5 years. He mixes and freezes ingredients
worth £2, loads his barrow, mixes a further £2 worth of ingredients,
puts them in the freezer, and prepares to set off. Just as he is about
to leave, his supplier looks in to leave another £15 worth of
ingredients, telling Antonio that he can pay later.

What is the financial position of Antonio's business now? What
does he own? He has two kinds of assets: fixed assets (the barrow
and machinery), which he will keep and use, and current assets
(his stocks and the remainder of the cash), which will be used up
and replenished in the course of making and selling his product.
With £15 extra stock on his shelves his assets now total £115. The
sources, too, have been increased by the same amount; he now

has a creditor to whom he must pay £15 before very long. This new source is therefore a liability, indicating an obligation on Antonio's part to pay out a sum of money of that amount at some time in the future. This contrasts with his original source, his own £100, which will not have to be paid out to anyone while the business lasts, and is, therefore, ownership capital, which remains permanently in the business. The balance sheet now reads as Table 3 shows.

TABLE 3. ANTONIO'S ICE-CREAM
Balance Sheet as at 1 May 19.. (2.30 p.m.)

Sources	£	Assets	£	£
Ownership capital	100	Fixed assets:		
		Machinery	80	
Liabilities:		Barrow	2	
Creditors	15		——	82
		Current assets:		
		Stock	20	
		Cash	13	
			——	33
	£115			£115

We should note in passing that Antonio's stock is now in three places: on the shelf, in the freezer, and on his barrow. Accountants recognize that stock can be of three kinds—raw material, work-in-progress, and finished goods. Annual company accounts seldom distinguish between these three forms of stock, but the distinction will be important in later discussions on stock valuation and budgeting.

Antonio has spent his savings and prepared his product because of his conviction that he can go out and sell it. When he gets to the street corner he is stopped by the manager of a sea-front café who has sampled the recipe and is willing to buy all the first batch. He says to Antonio: "Take it round to the café and I'll drop a cheque in tomorrow." Antonio leaves the ice-cream and an invoice for £6.

Another asset has now entered Antonio's balance sheet. It is a current asset, having come into the business in the course of the daily cycle of operations. It is a most important current asset, and one which only the marketing process can create. It is called debtors. Debtors are created when a business transfers some of its stock to customers, i.e. when it delivers the goods. In a cash sale the debtor extinguishes the debt immediately by paying for the goods he receives as he receives them. This is why we would not find debtors in the balance sheet of a small retailing business which sold only for cash. But most businesses sell on credit. Even a retail business of any size will have approved monthly accounts, and so will garages and filling stations.

When Antonio left his ice-cream at the café, he created a debtor worth £6 to him. He "owned" a debt receivable—an expectation of cash to be received in the future—of £6. But he parted with stock which had cost him only £2, so that there was a net increase of £4 in the total assets of his business. In accounting terms, it is essentially the transformation of stock into debtors that brings profit, or income, into the business.

Antonio can now claim to have earned £4 profit. (A moment's thought will show that this is not necessarily clear profit. He may have to pay rent on the room he used, and there will be an electricity bill. To the extent that he has begun to use services for which he will pay later, Antonio has incurred accrued charges, which are the costs of services used but not yet invoiced by the supplier or paid for by the user. At the moment, Antonio's accrued charges are probably negligible, and since accountants should not waste time recording negligible amounts, we will leave accrued charges out of his balance sheet for the present.) This £4 profit is his; it can be added to his original £100 as an increase in the permanent capital of the business. This increase is an example of a source of finance which accountants call reserves.

Reserves are retained earnings and do not necessarily exist in the form of cash. Nor are profits the same as cash. It is true that profit exists as cash at the moment when customers pay for goods received, but it does not remain in that form. The cash in a business is continually being used (in meeting expenses or buying assets), and there is no reason at all, other than pure chance, why the cash inside a business at a particular point of time should equal the profit it claims to have made during a period of time. The balance sheet on p. 26 shows this clearly. Antonio has earned £4 profit but he owns £13 in cash (which is what will be left of his original capital when the cheques he issued have been banked). His profit does not exist in the form of cash because he has not yet been paid for the goods sold. He can confidently expect to be paid, however, and rightly claims that the profit is already financing the business.

The significance to a marketing man of the distinction between reserves, profits, and cash is largely in the avoidance of "over-trading", which we shall discuss later in connection with liquidity.

If Antonio has a surplus of cash in the business not needed for day-to-day payments, he can put it into an investment to earn interest. A deposit account at the bank would be one such possibility. In so doing, Antonio would be introducing another kind of asset into his balance sheet, a current asset if the investment were short-term or a fixed or non-current asset if it were in some more permanent form.

Current assets are sometimes called circulating assets because they circulate in the course of the business cycle. Cash is spent on stock, which becomes debtors, who eventually pay cash and so enable the business to buy more stock. The whole cycle depends solely on the willingness of customers to buy.

Antonio's balance sheet now looks like Table 4.

This covers Antonio's assets so far. We can now turn to his sources of finance, which developed considerably during his first 6 months in business. This was due entirely to the fact that he judged his markets well, selling successfully both in bulk to cafés and from the barrow to trippers. During July he took over the ice-cream van and trade of another ice-cream vendor who had decided to retire from business, and, with the aid of a private mortgage, bought some premises in which to house more stocks and equipment. In August he borrowed a sum of money with which to acquire a milk-delivery business. He did this partly to

TABLE 4. ANTONIO'S ICE-CREAM

Balance Sheet as at 1 May 19·· (3.30 p.m.)

Sources	£	£	Assets	£	£
Ownership capital:			Fixed Assets:		
Original capital	100		Machinery	80	
Reserves	4		Barrow	2	
		104			82
Creditors		15			
			Current assets:		
			Stock	18	
			Debtors	6	
			Cash	13	
					37
		£119			£119

offset seasonal variations with a regular winter trade and partly to provide an outlet for a new ice-cream mixture which could be frozen to any desired consistency in a domestic refrigerator and which could therefore be delivered with the morning milk. Towards the end of October, the cash position of his business was temporarily stretched, and a bank overdraft had become necessary. Nevertheless, Antonio had promised himself a cruise in the spring, which he expected to pay for out of the profits of the business.

Table 5 shows Antonio's balance sheet on 31 October, reflecting the changes which these events brought about in his financial position, and illustrating further items which appear in business accounts.

This balance sheet would need further adjustment before it gives the "true and fair view" required by company legislation. One important item which has not yet been inserted is the depreciation of fixed assets. This is usually worked out annually, and most company accounts show separately the original cost figure, the depreciation to date, and the net amount which actually figures in the balance sheet. Antonio's accountant has not yet discussed with him what the depreciation should be, but they will certainly decide

TABLE 5. ANTONIO'S ICE-CREAM
Balance Sheet as at 31 October 19..

Sources	£	£
Ownership capital:		
Original capital	100	
Reserves	2204	2304
Long-term liabilities:		
Mortgage (6% for 10 yr)	1000	
Loan (6½% for 3 yr)	1900	
Future tax	1500	4400
Current liabilities:		
Bank overdraft	76	
Creditors	300	
Accrued charges	50	
Proposed withdrawal of profit	150	576
		£7280

Assets	£	£
Goodwill, at cost		1000
Fixed assets (at cost):		
Land and buildings	4000	
Plant and machinery	400	
Vehicles	1000	5400
Current assets:		
Stock	180	
Debtors	670	
Cash	30	880
		£7280

this before the first year's results are reported next May. Depreciation will be explained below on p. 35.

Before we look at the sources of finance, we should notice one more kind of asset which Antonio acquired during his expansion. This was goodwill. Goodwill appears in the balance sheet of a business when it has acquired another business, and has had to pay more for the physical or tangible assets of the newly acquired business than they were worth in themselves. The price paid over and above the market value of the assets as such is called goodwill, and is paid in recognition of the fact that the business connection taken over with the land and buildings, etc., also has a value. This value lies in the expectation that customers will continue to support the new owner, who will continue to make profits through selling to them. Goodwill is an intangible asset, and because a certain amount of commercial risk attaches to its value, its cost is usually transferred from the balance sheet to the profit and loss account as soon as there are sufficient sales to absorb it. (This procedure should be much clearer by the end of chapter 3.)

Sources of finance in a business are essentially of two different kinds: ownership capital, which will never have to be paid out while the business lasts, and liabilities, which will have to be paid out at some future date. Long-term liabilities will not have to be met until after the 12 months following the balance sheet date, but current liabilities will be due for payment during the ensuing 12 months. This groups the sources under the three main headings shown on p. 27.

Antonio's permanent capital of £2304 is made up of his original capital of £100 plus his reserves, which have now grown from £4 to £2204. The capital of a limited liability company is held in the form of shares, and at the top of the list of sources in a company balance sheet you would see some such heading as "Issued share capital of X Ltd.", or "Share capital authorized and issued" or "Capital and capital reserves".

Shares in a limited company may be either preference or ordinary shares. The difference lies in the differing rights of each class of shareholder to share in the distribution of profit, called dividend. Preference shares carry a fixed rate of dividend, based on the book value of the shares, and dividend at this rate will be due whether profits are large or small. Preference shares may be cumulative, which means that the right to an annual dividend may be carried forward should current profits be insufficient to allow payment. Ordinary shares, however, bear dividends only at the discretion of the directors. They are likely to vary between good years and lean years, and purchase of ordinary shares is therefore something of a risk. The dividend on ordinary shares (sometimes called equities, because they claim the balance of distributable profits) could be zero, or could be around, say, 40%.

A consistently low yield makes a company's shares unpopular in the money market, and is the inevitable result of not selling well. "Selling well" means selling goods of controlled cost at appropriate prices in sufficient quantities to yield a satisfactory profit. Every function inside the company, and many forces outside it, contribute in different ways to achieving successful sales, and have different claims to a share in the sales £. The contribution of the ordinary shareholder is to place his capital at risk in order to get the business started and keep it going, and the potentially high dividends are some compensation for the risks he takes.

Antonio's capital is very much at risk in his ice-cream venture. He stands to lose everything or make a fortune, which would put him in the "ordinary shares" class if his business became a limited liability company.

Reserves need a little more explanation. Company balance sheets may contain reserves of two kinds: revenue reserves and capital reserves. Revenue reserves, as we saw, are the retained profits or earnings which accumulate year by year inside a successful business. They may be shown as general reserves or earmarked for a particular reason, e.g. depreciation, debt redemption, contingencies. Directors of companies will divide up revenue reserves in this way mainly to indicate to shareholders that there are likely to be future claims on the business other than the shareholders' own legitimate claims to dividends. It is important to remember that none of these reserves necessarily represent cash; cash holdings are shown on the assets side.

But there are also capital reserves. These are not the savings that result from sales; they come into the business in other ways. If Antonio found that he had a machine in his books at £20 which he did not need, and managed to sell it for £25, the difference of £5 would be shown as a capital reserve and would increase his assets by £5. (In fact, two classes of asset are affected in this transaction; can you say which, and by how much, before you look at the answer at the foot of the page?)* Or if Antonio became a company and wished to issue £500 worth of shares, he might, if the shares were in great demand, sell them for £525. This is alled selling shares at a premium, and the £25 premium would be s 10wn as a capital reserve under the heading "Premium on shares iss ied". The nominal amount of the shares would remain £500, and v ould be the amount on which the dividend percentage would be alculated. Capital reserves do not always bring in cash. Som imes companies revalue their land and buildings, usually to bri g the book values more into line with the increased benefits of wnership. This creates a capital reserve and gives a better approximation of the ownership stake in the business. But the revalued figure does not claim to be the market value of the property (which has no actual market value until a prospective purchaser agrees a price for it). Nor, obviously, does this revaluation bring any cash into the company; it is a book entry only. The introduction of intangibles into the balance sheet (like assumed higher property values) is always done very cautiously.

Reserves are always part of the ownership capital. They may be amounts earmarked for future needs, but at the balance-sheet date they do not cover any known liability. In this respect they are different from provisions, which are sums set aside to meet known liabilities of unknown amount, e.g. future tax, pensions, amounts likely to be unrecovered from bad debtors. The phrase "depreciation provision" is often used, though strictly speaking these sums

* Fixed assets decrease by £20 and cash increases by £25, making a net increase of £5 in the asset values.

are not provisions, since they involve no claims on the assets from outside parties.

These then are the main ownership sources of finance listed in a balance sheet:

> **Share capital**
> > (Cumulative) preference shares (% dividend stated).
> > Ordinary shares.
>
> *plus* **Capital reserves**
> > General (e.g. surpluses on sale of capital equipment).
> > Premium on shares issued.
> > Etc.
>
> *plus* **Revenue reserves**
> > Retained profits.
> > Depreciation provisions.
> > Reserves for contingencies.
> > Etc.
>
> *equals* **Total owners' equity** (or "net worth" or "net share-holders' interest").

This list shows some of the possible ways in which Antonio's original £100 can grow as a result of successful trading. However, as we saw, he got financial help from other, non-ownership, sources, in order to take his business opportunities more quickly; in other words, he incurred liabilities. The main long-term liabilities in company balance sheets are loans of various kinds and future tax provisions. A common form of loan is the debenture, a loan made for an agreed period at a fixed rate of interest. Frequently they run for 20 years, and interest rates depend on the state of the money market at the time of issue. Company balance sheets contain entries like these:

> $3\frac{1}{2}$% first mortgage debenture stock, 1965–75 (secured).
> $6\frac{3}{4}$% unsecured loan stock, 1984–9.

Mortgage debentures confer on the debenture-holder a legal charge on the assets of the borrowing company, as security for the loan. But loans may also be unsecured. Whether secured or not, the debenture-holder is entitled to his interest before a profit is declared. However substantial his loan, he does not participate in profits or have any say in the management of the company.

We noted in Antonio's last balance sheet that he had taken out a mortgage and borrowed a further sum presumably without security. Almost certainly these would be private advances, since financial institutions rarely lend to a sole trader who has yet to establish himself. In each case, the balance sheet showed the term of the loan and the rate of interest. This information is important because it reveals the timing of the redemption of the loan and the interest charges due until redemption. All this requires cash, and Antonio will need to make sure that cash is available when the time comes.

The final item of long-term liability was tax. This is a provision, a sum set aside for a known liability the exact amount of which has not yet been precisely defined. Antonio is making a good profit, but he cannot put all of this into the "retained earnings" class and claim it as his own. A substantial part will eventually be claimed in taxes, and Antonio calculates that the taxes will be roughly £1500. He will not have to pay the tax until required to do so by current tax regulations, which will call for it on 1 January following the end of the tax year in which his financial year ends. This will give Antonio the use of the tax money for several months. Hence, "future tax" can rightly be called a source of finance. But, once again, Antonio must be careful to have the money ready at the due date.

This brings us to the current liabilities. By now it must be obvious what these are: short-term obligations that a business must expect to meet within 12 months of the balance-sheet date, often within 2 or 3 months. Common examples are creditors (mainly suppliers of materials received but not yet paid for), accrued charges (the cost of services rendered to the company but not yet paid for), tax (incurred on profits made earlier and soon due to be paid over to the inland revenue), and bank overdrafts. Typically, these are short-term advances which the bank will make to relieve a temporary shortage of cash; but some companies, by arrangement, run overdrafts for long periods. A final current liability could be dividends declared but not yet paid out. These amounts are withdrawals of what would otherwise be part of the ownership capital, the retained earnings. Antonio intends to withdraw £150. This liability is a policy or discretionary one. Antonio as owner of the business is free to withdraw profit as he thinks fit.

We have now described all the items commonly found in company balance sheets and the next thing to do is to determine a value for each.

Putting a Value to Balance-sheet Items

We have been putting values to Antonio's sources of finance and his assets without much apparent difficulty. Why then are there problems in valuing balance-sheet items? And why should marketing people be concerned with these problems, which rightly belong to accountants?

The answer is that anyone who wants to analyse a company's financial position needs to understand what lies behind the figures, why there are alternative ways of valuing assets, and how accounting practices can vary from company to company. This does not mean that financial reports are compiled in an arbitrary way or that there are no commonly held criteria which allow for comparability, but it does mean that absolutely objective financial measurement is impossible, despite the need to choose a precise figure in the end. Before drawing inferences from accounting reports—and the reports would be useless if no one ever drew any inferences from them—it is as well to be aware of the elements from which the figures can be calculated, and of the areas where judgement influences the final choice of values.

As far as balance-sheet figures are concerned, the main problem areas are the assets and the owners' equity. Obligations outside the company are usually the subject of clear agreement with the creditor concerned. For example, Antonio knows how much he borrowed from the mortgagor, and would be able to put this amount in his balance sheet without if's and but's. Quite how the mortgage lies, as between capital and interest, could, of course, be debated, but the mortgagor will presumably give Antonio periodic statements of account, which Antonio must accept.

Difficulties do arise, however, with the valuation of assets. The general convention among accountants is to enter capital acquisitions in the books at cost, but only at the moment of acquisition would the balance-sheet figure reflect the market value of the asset. Generally speaking, the longer an asset has been on the company's books, the less will its balance-sheet value correspond with its current market value. Sometimes a company may feel that a more appropriate relationship should be re-established between ownership funds and fixed asset values as reported in the balance sheet, and this will perhaps lead to a revaluation of land and buildings if property values have risen since acquisition.* Even so, the balance-sheet value is not a market value. Nor should it be. The asset is not in the market: it is by definition being kept for use.

When it comes to a piece of machinery, even the acquisition cost may be debated. The price at which it is invoiced from the supplier is a good start, but delivery and installation charges are often added in, and these may include labour costs of the firm's own work force. The extent to which the capital cost includes these items may depend on the tax advantage to be gained from claiming them as capital rather than revenue expense, or on the extent to which the company wishes to write off the charges during the current accounting period or defer them to a later period. In any event, the need for judgement may blur the limits of the ownership claim.

Problems arise with asset valuation because expenditure on assets (as distinct from expenditure on current costs like rent) has to be spread over the accounting periods over which the assets are

---

* When Marks & Spencer Ltd. revalued their property in 1964, the independent valuers pointed out that while the capital expenditure incurred on acquiring the property had been very substantial, the benefits (of ownership) had been even greater.

used up. The crux of the problem is this: which operating periods should bear the cost of the assets? The year of purchase should obviously not carry the full cost since this would understate, or even wipe out, the profit to be claimed during this period. But if not the year of purchase, which years? Antonio's ice-cream machinery was expected to last for 5 years, so he would hold the cost in an asset account and release it to the operating accounts during these 5 years by annual amounts called depreciation charges. As each instalment of the capital cost is charged out, the value shown in the balance sheet drops by the same amount. But how much of the cost should go to each year? There are several methods of calculating the annual amounts and each method gives a different annual charge and hence a different residual value in each year's balance sheet.

Three methods in common use are the straight-line method, the reducing-balance method, and the production-unit method. The straight-line method divides total cost by number of years of usefulness and allots an equal portion of cost to each year of use. The reducing-balance method applies a constant percentage to the balance of cost outstanding, and in so doing absorbs more depreciation in the early years than in later years. This is justified partly because the asset is likely to yield more benefit in its earlier years than in later years; also because by this method depreciation charges will drop as maintenance and repair charges tend to increase, so helping to stabilize costs over the years. The production-unit method predicts the total output of the asset, and allocates both output and cost to the different years of asset life in the same proportion, again matching costs (depreciation charge) with benefits.

The figures needed for a depreciation calculation are: the initial cost, the disposal value, if any, the useful life, and the basis of apportionment. Every one of these figures involves a judgement: there can be no absolutely correct answer. Antonio knows what he paid for his machinery, but not how long it will last, nor what he will get for it when it is no further use to him. On what basis he should charge its costs to his takings over the years is a matter for him to decide. No one looking at his balance sheet would know the assumptions he made.

The situation is further complicated by the fact that the phasing of depreciation depends not only on wear and tear, but also on obsolescence, i.e. the process of becoming outmoded. If better ice-cream making machinery comes out, Antonio may find it more profitable to get rid of his older machinery and install new equipment. In accounting terms, the old equipment would in that case suffer depreciation by obsolescence. Antonio would write off the outstanding value as shown in the balance sheet (less any sum he could get for the machinery on disposal) and the extra depreciation charge would be due to obsolescence. Naturally, the obsolescence of plant due to the availability of better plant does not in itself provide the cash wherewith to buy the new plant.

The process of depreciation is one of allocation rather than valuation. It follows that the depreciated values of fixed assets shown in balance sheets represent the acquisition costs not yet allocated, or "booked out", as manufacturing and trading costs, and do not in any sense represent what these assets would fetch if put up for sale. This is in accordance with the general view of a balance sheet as a statement showing the sources of funds and the assets to which these funds have been applied. A half-consumed asset should not claim to represent more than half the funds originally invested in it.

Company balance sheets often show the acquisition cost of fixed assets held in the business, the total depreciation to date, and the net figure carried forward into the next accounting period. Notes to the accounts often show disposals and new acquisitions, and sometimes outstanding capital expenditure commitments. All these figures give an indication of the extent to which a company is redeploying its financial resources to meet longer term demand for its products.

Of the current assets, stock is the one bringing most valuation problems. The value attached to stock on hand at the end of an accounting period has a direct bearing on the profit figure claimed or that period, as every trader knows. Given the cost of a barrow-load of ice-cream, the lower the stock value at the end of the day the higher the cost of stock to be put against the day's takings. Before starting to make his own ice-cream, Antonio might have bought someone else's, and a typical afternoon's trading might have been:

Bought 600 bricks at 4*d*. each: £10
Sold 480 bricks at 6*d*. each: £12

The cost of the 120 unsold bricks was £2 and the profit calculation becomes:

	£
Opening stock	Nil
Purchases	10
	10
Less Closing stock	2
Cost of goods sold	8
Sales value	12
Profit	£4

If the saleable closing stock, through spoliage, free gifts, or theft were valued at only £1, the cost of goods sold would be £9 and the profit only £3. The stock figure in fact has the effect of dividing expenditure (in this case, on purchases) between the current period and future periods. Since it divides expenditure, it also divides profit.

The usual accounting procedure is to value stock at cost or market value, whichever is the lower. This is the conservative view, which generally writes off losses early, and avoids claiming a profit potential which is unlikely to materialize. If Antonio's customers all decided that in future 2*d*. was the most they would pay for an ice-cream brick, Antonio's balance sheet at the end of the afternoon would show stock at £1 (120 at 2*d*.), and he would prudently claim only £3 profit for the afternoon's trading. The £1 difference in profit would be due to the expense of a stock write-down. Again, if Antonio miscounted his closing stock and called it 150 bricks, he might show closing stock at £2 10s. and claim £4 10s. profit. In a simple case like this he could, of course, reconcile cash takings with stock no longer in his possession, but in a business of any size, this is not possible, and the closing stock value remains a key figure in determining profit.

In practice, it can be difficult to say what the market value of the stock is; as we saw with property, you can never be absolutely certain of the market value until a buyer tells you what he will pay. This does not matter, of course, as long as the likely minimum market value remains above cost. But costs can be complicated, too. Different batches of the same item may come into stock at different prices, and it can be a costly clerical task to keep a continuous record of how much is in stock at what purchase price. If an attempt at an "actual" purchase price is thought worth while, an assumption has to be made as to which goods are in stock, those purchased earlier or those purchased most recently. When prices are fluctuating, these alternatives can give different stock valuations, and therefore different profit figures. We shall look at this problem in more detail in the next chapter.

Debtors arise through the submission of invoices to credit customers. It is theoretically simple to total the unpaid invoices at a given date, but some adjustment has usually to be made for bad or doubtful debtors. There are various ways of reaching a bad debts provision. Each account may be scrutinized in detail, and with knowledge of the customer's paying habits and ability (helped by scrutiny of his accounts if they are available), a decision can be made as to the likelihood of recovering all or part of the debt. But this takes time. In a firm with thousands of credit accounts, it may be possible to correlate actual bad debts with annual credit sales or total debtors outstanding, or, as a refinement, with debtors outstanding listed by age of debt, as shown in Table 6.

TABLE 6

Age of debts	£	Estimated % not collectible	Bad debts allowance (£)
Current	150,000	1	1,500
Less than 1 month overdue	20,000	1·5	300
1–2 months overdue	8,000	4	320
2–3 months overdue	4,000	10	400
Over 3 months overdue	2,000	30	600
	£184,000		£3,120

The figure for debtors is therefore another area where there is scope for judgement in the final choice of figure to be reported in the balance sheet.

At the end of the list of current assets comes cash, and here at least the balance-sheet figure is straightforward. There are always cheques in the pipeline, of course, and remittances in the post might or might not qualify for inclusion in the total. A company can adopt whatever rules it sees fit for counting cash at balance-sheet date provided it applies them consistently.

Despite the need for judgement in valuing assets, balance sheets can generally be relied on to give a meaningful summary of the financial position of a business, and a series of balance sheets will effectively summarize the movements in financial sources, claims, and uses. What has been said about the need for judgement in compiling balance sheets is intended as an antidote to the view that money figures have a compelling accuracy about them which cannot be gainsaid. It is certainly not intended to encourage the reader to have no faith in company accounts, which would amount to attacking an important part of the financial control system.

The judgements made about asset valuation and the division of costs between time periods will all affect the final profit figure. Profits appropriated to dividends or tax are precisely calculated, "cashed", and paid out; the retained profit is the residue, which

finally balances the balance sheet. The determination of profit
brings many problems in itself, and this takes us to the next
chapter.

Summary

A balance sheet summarizes the financial position of a business
at a point of time. It shows how much finance there is in the business, where it came from, what financial claims are likely to arise
in the future, and in what way the finance is being used.

The main sources of finance are ownership capital (original
capital and retained earnings), long-term loans, future tax liabilities, and current sources (overdrafts, trade creditors, etc.). These
sources have different claims on the business which, if the business
is to continue, must be met as they fall due.

Finance is expended in purchasing assets and meeting expenses.
Assets are things purchased but not wholly used up at balance-
sheet date; part at least of the benefit of ownership has not yet
expired, and putting a value to the unexpired benefit is a matter of
judgement within the limits of accounting conventions. Assets are
of two main kinds: fixed (to be kept and used) and current (to
circulate in the business cycle). Current assets circulate through
the marketing process, which aims to satisfy customers and generate profits.

Total sources always equal total assets; a change in total sources
must involve a corresponding change in total assets and vice versa.

Balance sheets relate to the company as a whole and give
stewardship information to the owners of the business or other
financial backers. They are also useful to investment analysts,
bankers, creditors, and internal management—to anyone, in short,
who is interested in the financial health of the business. For
marketing people, the financial position shown in the balance
sheet is a measure of the strength and stability which supports
future marketing effort.

CHAPTER 3

How Profitable
were our Sales?

THIS chapter is about profit and loss accounts. They are different from balance sheets in that they summarize a series of financial events which have occurred during a period of time, while balance sheets describe how things are at a point of time.

Profit and loss accounts are sometimes called income statements, and that is precisely what they are. The term "income" means, not total receipts of cash from customers (this is better described as revenue) but the difference between sales value of goods sold and the total cost to the business of effecting those sales. Another word for sales less total cost of sales is, of course, profit. This may seem to be a different use of the word income from its use in relation to a private individual; an individual's income is generally considered to be the total cash he receives. However, the tax authorities allow even private individuals to set certain basic costs against their receipts, and it is the residual amount so arrived at that is called income and taxed as such.

As far as a business is concerned, it is important to note that income has no necessary connection with the inflow of cash. Income is earned when something extra is added to the ownership stake in the business, i.e. to the retained earnings. An inflow of cash may not do this; it may be accompanied by a drop in some other asset (as when debtors pay up) or by an increase in a liability (as when an investor hands over a sum of money on loan).

Income, then, is the profit made by a business. The profit and loss account, or income statement, records the financial events which, taken together, provide a measure of the income realized by the firm over a stated period. While a business may derive a small income here and there by investing spare cash or selling surplus fixed assets, its essential income is derived from profitable sales. The profit and loss account answers a question which must deeply concern all marketing people: how profitable were our sales?

In some circumstances it is simple to determine profit. The village garden fête presents no problems. Money is collected at the gate, the bills are paid, and what is left is claimed as profit. The determination of profit is simple in this case because the garden fête is an isolated venture. Financially speaking, it comes to an end when the profit is handed over to the organizers. The same thing could be done with a business if it were taken over its whole life. The total cash which the owners got out of it (dividends and net cash on liquidation) less the cash they originally put in would equal the total profit made by the company during its existence. But such a procedure would be useless for a business. The managers and shareholders want to know how well they are doing at fairly frequent intervals (a crucial factor in the control process), and so the life of the business is chopped up into short, regular spans of time called accounting periods. It is the accountant's job to compute the sales revenues earned in each period and match with them the expenses incurred during the same period.

While the allocation of expenses to periods of time is one of the central problems of accountancy, this does not mean that costs and profits are arbitrary figures computed only in accordance with managerial whims. There is a large measure of objective agreement on what profit figures mean, and to illustrate this we shall adopt the same plan as with balance sheets: to explain the items commonly found in profit and loss accounts and then discuss how a value is put on each.

But first let us look at a period of business activity and see how the events lead up to a profit and loss account. We can go back to Antonio, who, as we saw in Chapter 2, established his business firmly during its first 6 months. He began by selling ice-cream from a barrow, took over another ice-cream business, and eventually became a wholesale dairyman, selling a new product of his own invention to other deliverymen. The sales of all lines handled came to £6750. In all, he bought ingredients and dairy produce in bulk worth £2380. He avoided large stocks, both to save space and to conserve his liquidity (this will be explained in Chapter 4), and had only £180 worth of stock on the shelf on 31 October. Other purchases were land and buildings, machinery, and motor-vehicles; these items represented capital expenditure on fixed assets, and as such would not be shown in the profit and loss account. They were in fact listed in the balance sheet on p. 27 (Table 5), because their usefulness and their cost will be spread over many accounting periods, not just the 6 months we are thinking about at the moment. There were other current expenses: electricity, wages, motor-vehicle running costs, packaging materials, office expenses, and so on.

The profit and loss account (Table 7) shows how these events were recorded. Notice how the report starts with the value of sales made during the period, sets out all the expenses incurred in meeting customer needs, arrives at a net profit figure (we could loosely call this "clear profit", with all expenses taken into the reckoning), and then shows how this profit is disposed of or appropriated. In this way, receipts from sales are fully accounted for. A profit and loss account, like any other accounting report, should be set out in the form most helpful to those who are going to read it and act on it. This guiding principle apart, there are no hard and fast rules on how to draw up such a statement. As far as limited companies are concerned, however, the distinction should be made between the profit and loss account published for the shareholders, and the internal profit and loss account prepared for management, which is much more detailed.

The published profit and loss accounts of companies are simple in format. They usually begin with the trading profit (often called "operating profit"), and give the sort of information shown in Table 8. At present, companies are not obliged to tell even their shareholders what their sales value, or turnover, is. There is a

TABLE 7. ANTONIO'S ICE-CREAM

Profit and Loss Account for the 6 Months ending 31 October

	£	£	£
Sales			6750
Less:			
Cost of goods sold:			
Opening stock		Nil	
Purchases		2380	
		2380	
Less Closing stock		180	
			2200
Gross profit			4550
Less:			
Wages		180	
Overheads:			
Electricity	50		
Administration	150		
Distribution	271		
Loan Interest	45		
		516	
			696
Net profit before tax			3854
Less Provision for tax			1500
Net profit after tax			2354
Less Proposed withdrawal of profit			150
Net profit retained in business			£2204

traditional secrecy about this figure, but a growing number of companies see no point in this, and are quite happy to tell the world the value of their sales. At the time of writing there are moves afoot to compel disclosure of turnover.* And why not?

* The Report of the Company Law Committee (the Jenkins Committee) recommended in 1962 that annual accounts should be required to disclose turnover unless the directors were satisfied that disclosure would be harmful. The Committee also recommended that legislation on disclosure should make no distinction between public and private companies. If these proposals were embodied in new company legislation, balance sheet, turnover, and profit figures would be available to the public in respect of limited liability companies of any size.

TABLE 8. ABC COMPANY LTD.

Profit and Loss Account for the Year to 30 June 19..

	This year		Previous Year	
	£	£	£	£
Profit on trading		151,800		132,200
After charging:				
Depreciation	40,100		33,000	
Directors' emoluments	5,000		3,800	
Add:				
Income from investments:				
Trade investments	4,600		1,400	
Government securities	3,200		2,300	
Short-term deposits	3,100		2,800	
		10,900		6,500
		162,700		138,700
Deduct:				
Interest payable on:				
Bank overdraft	6,300		3,200	
Long-term loan stock	4,400		5,300	
		10,700		8,500
Net profit before tax		152,000		130,200
Corporation tax (40%)	60,800		52,080	
Net dividend	30,100		28,220	
Income tax deductible from gross dividend	21,100		19,900	
Total appropriations		112,000		100,200
Retained profit added to reserves		£42,000		£30,000

Items Commonly Found in Profit and Loss Accounts

Most of the items found in the detailed profit and loss statements used by management will be familiar to people engaged in the daily round of business life. However, it will be helpful to refer briefly to the main items and the categories in which they are usually grouped.

The first item is the gross amount which customers have paid or acknowledge to be due in exchange for the goods or services marketed by the company, i.e. sales. It is a good practice for this item not to include other receipts such as interest on investments, which are not the result of the company's marketing effort. Revenue of this kind, of course, contributes to profit, but is best brought in as shown in Table 8, after the trading profit has been clearly stated. Obviously, this is not true of finance companies, whose marketing effort aims to bring in dividends and interest. For manufacturing and trading companies, the revenue aimed at is that produced by the circulation of its current assets, and this is the item with which to head up the profit and loss account.

Which item actually heads up the statement does not, of course, matter; as we said earlier, the convenience of the users should alone decide how the information is presented. Shareholders are presumed to be interested in the trading profit, so company profit and loss accounts usually begin with this. Internal profit and loss accounts will usually begin with either sales or costs, depending on the assumptions made about which of these items the recipient is most interested in. But most managers and directors look first at the trading profit, and it is odd that one never sees, in textbooks or in reality, a profit and loss statement with the profit (or loss) put at the head of the sheet. "If we did that", say the accountants, "they'd look no further."

The order we are assuming here is: sales, costs, profit. The next item, then, is the cost of goods sold. Marketing people have a keen interest in the cost of what they are selling, and they are sometimes puzzled by the way in which accountants seem to manipulate costs in respect of the same article. And they will certainly feel let down if they find a competitor claiming to produce the same article at lower cost.

The nature of cost of goods sold is more complex in a manufacturing business than in a purely trading business, so it will be convenient to consider it separately in each type of business.

The cost of goods sold in a retailing, wholesaling, or factoring business is broadly the purchase price of those goods. If no stocks are held, then purchases in an accounting period equal cost of goods sold. But if, as is normal, there are stocks, then the cost of goods sold during a period of time is the difference between opening stock at the beginning of the period plus purchases during the period (= cost of all goods available for sale during this time), and the closing stock at the end of the period. This calculation was shown in Antonio's profit and loss account (Table 7), p. 44. By this calculation, the assumption is that all goods not in stock at the end of the period have been sold to customers.

There are, of course, other reasons why stocks are depleted: free samples, deterioration, theft, or internal consumption, for example. Stock withdrawal for reasons other than sale needs to be carefully recorded, or the cost of goods sold figure will be distorted. This will then distort the gross profit figure, although the net profit figure will be the same in the end. The cost of issuing free samples, stock deterioration, and so on are overhead charges, and will be deductions from gross profit made in the course of computing net profit before tax.

The simplified profit and loss accounts (Table 9) p. 48 show how segregation of stock issues for reasons other than sale to customers gives a different gross profit figure but does not affect net profit. The trader who does not bother to document free issues, internal consumption, etc., will perhaps wonder why he shows a lower gross margin than his competitor who does segregate non-sales issues. How much detailed stock recording a trader should do depends, as always, on the usefulness of the information gained from the records. In some companies, the value of free samples and so on may be too insignificant to record; in others, salesmen after free samples or demonstration models will be asked to fill up or sign a form, which is simply a way of transferring the amount involved from cost of goods sold account to an appropriate overhead expense account, and hence of improving the accuracy and significance of the gross profit ratio.

In a manufacturing company the cost of goods sold is not merely the cost of the material in the commodity, but of the manufacturing expenses incurred in converting the raw or semi-processed material to a new, saleable, product. These expenses are traditionally of two kinds: labour and overheads; these are added in one way or another to the cost of material or components

TABLE 9. EFFECT OF DIFFERENT COST OF GOODS SOLD CALCULATIONS
ON GROSS PROFIT AND NET PROFIT

Profit and Loss Account: Period X

	All stock issues assumed to be sales			Non-sales issues segregated		
	£	£	% on sales	£	£	% on sales
Sales		100			100	
Opening stock	60			60		
Purchases	80			80		
	140			140		
Closing stock	75			75		
Cost of goods issued from stock	65			65		
Less non-sales issues	—			6		
Cost of goods sold	——	65		——	59	
Gross profit		35	35		41	41
Wages	10			10		
Non-sales issues of goods	—			6		
Other overheads	5			5		
Total wages and overheads	——	15		——	21	
Net profit		£20	20		£20	20

worked on. As a result, saleable goods accumulate in the dispatch bay at a cost analogous to, but more complex than, the purchase price which might be paid for the same goods if they were bought out.

However, the arithmetic needed to arrive at cost of goods sold in a manufacturing company takes the same form as the basic stock calculation in a non-manufacturing firm; the difference is that it needs to be done three times, as there are three essential categories of stock in a manufacturing business: raw material, work-in-progress, and finished goods. The procedure is shown in

Table 10, which illustrates how the flow of costs during an accounting period eventually leads to a money value of cost of goods sold (which will be deducted from the sales revenue for the same period) and of the closing stocks (which will be held as assets in the period-end balance sheet, to be deducted from the sales revenue of future periods).

TABLE 10. CALCULATION OF COST OF GOODS SOLD IN A
MANUFACTURING BUSINESS

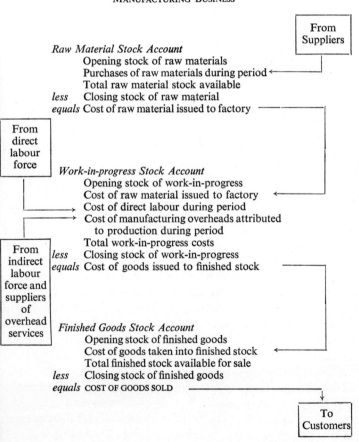

Direct labour costs are the wages and related expenses paid to or in respect of the people whose work involves the direct physical shaping or assembly of the product. Related expenses are, for example, employer's pension contributions or employer's national insurance contributions. Overheads are expenses not directly attributable to specific products or units of output, but which facilitate or benefit the business process. Manufacturing overheads benefit the manufacturing process, either generally (like the works manager's salary) or parts of it (like a section foreman's salary, or the power costs of running a particular machine). Anybody who has walked round a factory can easily visualize the overhead expenses incurred in manufacture: storekeeping, internal transport, repairs and maintenance, power, heat and lighting, production control and supervision costs, factory rent and rates, depreciation on plant and machinery.

So much for cost of goods sold. The other costs of running a business, which have all to be met before net profit can be declared, are usually classified as administrative costs, selling and distribution costs, and financial costs. All of these, too, are overheads. Administrative costs are the expenses of employing an administration and paying for what it does. This covers central management salaries and expenses, office costs (excluding factory and sales offices), company secretarial costs, and so on. Selling costs will need little explanation to the readers for whom this book is primarily intended; the salaries of such readers are selling overheads, as are salesmen's travelling expenses and commission, advertising and promotion costs, and marketing costs generally— the cost of doing all the things which this series of books says you should do to market successfully. Distribution costs are the costs of storing the finished product, physically moving it to the customer and of rendering him an invoice. Financial costs are the interest charges on borrowed capital and any other costs associated with changes in capital funds. Sometimes they are lumped in with administrative overhead, but are often set against investment income, as in the example on p. 45. Research and development costs are another kind of overhead expense. Depending on their significance to the company, they may be shown separately in the profit and loss account, or included in factory costs, or in general administrative overheads, if they are thought to benefit the company generally rather than the factory processes in particular. They may even be "capitalized", that is to say, held as an asset in the balance sheet, and not appear at all in the profit and loss account for the period in which they were incurred.

Putting a Value to Profit and Loss Account Items

The only way to answer the question "How profitable were our sales?" is to put a value on sales and on costs and compute the difference between them; if sales exceed costs, the resulting figure is the accounting measure of profit. In the following section of the book we shall explain some of the problems of accounting measurement and profit determination. This should help the reader to understand why arriving at a profit figure is as much a matter of informed opinion and judgement as of arithmetic.

A basic problem of cost ascertainment lies in the distinction between expenditure and expense, which is not simply a matter of words. Expenditure is incurred in buying, i.e. acquiring an asset or service. Expense is incurred in consuming the benefit of the asset or service for the purpose of earning revenue. Over the life of a business, most expenditures will become expenses, but in the shorter term, it frequently happens that expenditure can be incurred in one accounting period but not reckoned as expense until succeeding periods. This is because the benefit derived from the expenditure is not necessarily consumed during the same accounting period as that in which the expenditure was made. Depreciation of fixed assets is a good illustration of how this principle is applied. The effect on the profit and loss account is obvious. Since expenses, and not expenditures, are the costs incurred in achieving sales, it follows that some attempt must be made to match expenses with the sales they generate. This means matching the sales of a period with the expenses of the same period.

Unless this is done, the resulting profit figures will have little meaning.

Is not this concept routine for a salesman? "Our product may cost a bit more than competing products, but it will last you years longer." In accounting terms the salesman is saying "Purchase of our product will call for a higher initial expenditure than would competing products, but this won't make you incur higher expenses, since the benefits you will derive from it will be spread over many more accounting periods than the benefits from competing products. This will give you lower period expenses and higher period profits."

Expenditure, then, reflects the acquisition cost of a benefit, while expense reflects the expiry of a benefit. It follows that at the end of each accounting period, somebody must look at each expenditure and ask, "How much benefit has expired and how much is yet to come?" The cost of expired benefits is charged against sales revenue in the profit and loss account; the cost of unexpired benefits remains in the balance sheet and is the figure at which the assets are normally valued. Apportioning benefit to past and future periods is often a matter of judgement.

Depreciation charges are the obvious example of expenses calculated by apportioning benefit to past and future periods, but there are many others. Cost of goods sold is another good example. Manufacturing expenditure is tied up in stocks of finished goods, and does not become an expense until the period in which goods are sold. (Whether all manufacturing expenditure, or only part of it, should be added to the value of finished stocks is a debating point among accountants, and we shall return to this problem in a moment.) Another example of an expenditure that is not immediately an expense is goodwill.

What about advertising expense? This is incurred entirely for future benefits, i.e. the flow of orders which it should stimulate or maintain. But a direct relationship between money spent on advertising and the benefit derived from it is hard to establish despite such things as keyed advertisements; nor is it possible to apportion the expiry of the benefit to the accounting periods following the expenditure. Advertising expenditure is generally treated as an expense of the period in which it is incurred. Monthly profit figures would be affected by any time-lags between advertising expenditure and inflow of orders, but during a full year the advertising costs incurred should bear a better relationship to orders obtained in the same year. Just to be awkward— what about an expensive, once-only advertising campaign mounted in the last fortnight of the financial year? Which year should take this expense, assuming that it will cause a significant drop in the reported profit, or even turn it into a loss, if charged against the year just ending?

One way to avoid an unfair charge to the operating profit would be to bring this unusual, non-recurring advertising expense into the profit-and-loss account between operating profit and net profit before tax. This would enable the reported operating profit to bear comparison with the operating profit for the previous year. But should it be written off at all? Why not hold it as an asset in the balance sheet, since the benefits are yet to come? Some people would argue that advertising costs are rather like training costs or the costs of hiring a consultant. They are "influential" costs—the costs of influencing other people, and the benefits are received in two stages: first, when the advertisers, or trainers, or consultants put out effort on behalf of the client to influence the human behaviour which the client wishes to control, and, secondly, when the people respond to that influence. The first benefit is visible and measurable, but the second cannot be measured or phased in financial terms. It seems common sense to recognize that when we ask an advertising agent to do something, the benefit expires when he has done it. The treatment of advertising expense actually adopted will, as always, depend on the purpose of the accounting report and the inferences which are likely to be drawn from it.

We said that expenditure is not the same thing as expense; nor is it the same thing as making a payment. An expenditure is incurred when an asset is acquired (i.e. delivered to the premises) or a service accepted. The acceptance of the asset or service creates a liability which is at some time met by a corresponding payment (assuming there is no trade-in of assets as part of the consideration). Payment may be made before, simultaneously with, or after acceptance of the asset or service, and is a detail which we leave to the cashier. The important thing to bear in mind is that neither payment nor expenditure are necessarily expenses. Expenses, the money value of used up assets or services, are calculated with optimum accuracy because the economic justification for using up assets and services in a business is that in so doing, sales are generated; this is why expenses should be attributed carefully to each accounting period so that they can be matched with the sales revenue realized in the same period. Only thus will a meaningful period-by-period profit indicator result.

With this matching concept in mind, we can get a better understanding of how each profit and loss account item is measured. The first item is sales. This is the usual terminology, but what it really means, of course, is deliveries. A sale is not complete until the goods have been handed over to the customer, or at least dispatched from the works or warehouse. Physical dispatches are accompanied by the preparation and dispatch of an invoice, the document which tells customers what they owe for the goods they are receiving. A total of the invoices rendered during a period, corresponding with dispatches made during the same period, and adjusted for returns, discounts, or other allowances to customers, will provide the sales figure for the periodic profit and loss statement. Occasionally there is friction at management meetings when the general manager looks hard at the sales manager and says, "Sales are down", whereupon the sales manager, who is netting orders at a great rate, glares at the works manager and says, "You mean, deliveries are down". Orders are not sales, in the revenue-earning sense of the term. Receipt of an order makes no difference to either the balance sheet or the profit and loss account, though it will probably do so in due course.

The cost of goods sold would be straightforward arithmetic but for one permanent feature of economic life: the rise and fall in purchase prices. Suppose you were in business selling wooden logs of a standard type. Each period you buy 20 logs and sell 20, keeping 60 in stock in case of unpredictable demands. You buy the logs for £5 each and sell them for £10 each. At first, everything is stable: the cost, the price, rate of purchase, rate of sale, and the level of stocks. Each period you have a profit and loss account like Table 11.

TABLE 11.

	£	£
Sales		200 (20 × £10)
Opening stock	300 (60 × £5)	
Purchases	100 (20 × £5)	
	——	
	400	
Less Closing stock	300 (60 × £5)	
	——	
Cost of goods sold		100
		——
Gross profit		£100

Now the purchase price begins to rise. (To study the effect of different variables in a situation of change it is a good plan to let the variables move one at a time and hold the rest constant: we shall often do this.) We start with period 1: conditions stable. In periods 2, 3, and 4 the purchase price rises by £1 per log each period and then flattens out again at £8 per log. What happens to the gross profit over those periods of rising price, assuming that selling price, stock levels, and purchase and sales volumes remain constant?

The problem hits you at the end of period 2 when you want to work out your profit and loss account. Sales are £200 as usual; opening stocks, the same as the closing stock figure shown in the last profit and loss account, are £300; purchases are £120 (20 × £6), giving a sub-total of £420. And then you go round the timber yard to take stock. During period 2 you took in 20 logs from your supplier as usual, noting that he was now charging you £6 per log instead of £5; as usual, you sold 20. It now occurs to you that in order to cost out your sales and value your stock, you need to know which 20 you sold and which 60 are in stock. Did you sell any or all of the £6 logs which came in during period 2? How many of them, if any, are left in stock?

In the absence of clear information there are a large number of possibilities. To simplify matters, you take two extreme assumptions: (a) that all the sales were of £6 logs, and (b) that all sales were of logs bought earlier at £5. Then you draw up two profit and loss accounts, one based on the first assumption, one based on the second (Table 12).

TABLE 12

Profit and Loss Account, Period 2

| | (a) Logs sold Cost £6 each | | (b) Logs sold Cost £5 each | |
	£	£	£	£
Sales		200		200
Opening stock	300		300	
Purchases	120		120	
	420		420	
Less Closing stock	300		320	
Cost of goods sold	——	120	——	100
Gross profit		£80		£100

On assumption (a) your profit has dropped from £100 in period 1 to £80 in period 2. On assumption (b) it has remained constant at £100 in both periods. So you sit back, puzzled. Which is right?

The answer, of course, is that neither assumption is right and neither is wrong. Both are valid and acceptable accounting conventions. The crux of the matter lies in the valuation of the closing stock, as you can see by comparing profit and loss accounts (a) and (b) above. Both statements are identical down to closing stock. But statement (a) assumes that of the 80 logs available for sale during period 2, customers took the most recent stocks and left the oldest stocks, which, valued at cost, came to £300. On this assumption, the last in were the first out, and this method of stock valuation is therefore known as the LIFO ("last-in, first-out") method. Statement (b) assumes that customers took the 20 logs which had been longest in stock, leaving in stock 40 logs which had cost £5 each (£200) plus the 20 logs recently purchased at £6 each (£120), giving a closing stock value of £320. This means that the *first* in were assumed to be the first out, so this method is known as the FIFO ("first-in, first-out") method.

What difference do these methods make? Let us look at the profit and loss accounts for periods 1–4, using LIFO stock valuations. This time we will put sales at the bottom, to simplify the presentation (Table 13).

TABLE 13

Profit and Loss Accounts

	Period 1	Period 2	Period 3	Period 4	Total, Periods 1–4
	£	£	£	£	£
Opening stock (LIFO)	300	300	300	300	300
Purchases	100	120	140	160	520
	400	420	440	460	820
Less Closing stock (LIFO)	300	300	300	300	300
Cost of goods sold	100	120	140	160	520
Sales	200	200	200	200	800
Gross profit	100	80	60	40	280

Table 13 shows that your timber yard has made £280 gross profit during periods 1–4 inclusive. Over the road you have a competitor whose costs, prices, rate of purchase, and sale and stock levels are identical with yours. He, too, has read about LIFO and FIFO, and happens to have plumped for FIFO, on the assumption that he sells off earlier stock first and leaves the later purchases in stock. This assumption certainly seems to square better with the physical reality. This is how his profit and loss accounts turn out for periods 1–4:

TABLE 14
Profit and Loss Accounts

	Period 1	Period 2	Period 3	Period 4	Total, Periods 1–4
	£	£	£	£	£
Opening stock (FIFO)	300	300	320	360	300
Purchases	100	120	140	160	520
	400	420	460	520	820
Less Closing stock (FIFO)	300	320	360	420	420
Cost of goods sold	100	100	100	100	400
Sales	200	200	200	200	200
Gross profit	100	100	100	100	400

Table 14 shows that, in identical trading conditions, at an identical rate of business, your competitor appears to have made 42% more profit than you have; £400 against your £280. "Moreover", he says, "I have valued my stock at the lower of cost or market value, as the accountants say you should." But so have you.

Your competitor is not, of course, really doing any better than you; he is merely delaying the effect of the rise in purchase prices, whereas you are adding it to your cost of goods sold straight away. Eventually, if the purchase price remains at £8, you are both bound to settle down again to the same rate of profit.

A moment's thought will remind you that your competitor is not accumulating any more cash, since he is buying and selling at the same prices as you. This could be a disadvantage of FIFO assumptions—that in conditions like these, shareholders or unions could be misled into thinking that there are higher profits available for distribution. Profits, to be shared, must first be turned into cash, and this is not always possible.

When your competitor claims these higher profits all he is saying is: "I am selling old stock which, some time ago, I bought at prices below today's prices." This is his assumption, whether or not it is physically true. Sooner or later the old stocks give out, and his profits fall to your level as he begins to sell (in fact or in theory) the more recent, more expensive purchases. What you are saying is: "I have left my old stock in the yard and am selling the new, more expensive stuff as it comes in." As things are, you will never sell the 60 logs you had in stock at the start of period 2, when your first higher-priced consignment came in. So you will never make the profit on those logs which your competitor claims to have made, which comes to 60 × £5, or £300.

Before you rush out to sell those 60 logs remember that price rises are only half the story. Prices rise, but they also fall. If LIFO assumptions produce an immediate drop in profit when purchase prices rise (assuming stable selling prices), they also produce an immediate rise in profit when purchase prices fall. Over the whole cycle of price movement, LIFO and FIFO will give the same profit total, with FIFO allowing a time-lag related to the rate of stockturn.

If both methods of stock valuation give the same answer in the end, why all this fuss? Does it matter which way stock is valued? Yes, it does matter, because marketing people need to understand and accept the cost/selling price policy by which they sell; because a salesman needs to recognize and limit the occasions when, for good marketing reasons, he sells at a loss; because, in the distributive trades, commodities are subject to sudden tax increases around budget day, a situation in which stock levels, rates of purchase and sale, costs, and selling prices have to be rapidly predicted and controlled, in a manner that will satisfy as many interests as possible.

There seem to be several good reasons in favour of LIFO, of which the main ones are:

1. LIFO tends to stabilize stock valuation and reported profits (since, in practice, selling prices will tend to climb with purchase prices).
2. LIFO produces a more up-to-date cost of goods sold figure, a figure which tends to focus attention on future stock replacement costs.
3. Since prices broadly tend to rise more than they fall, the lower profits reported by a LIFO system may tend to delay payment of income tax, though this advantage is problematical.

The different effects of alternative stock valuation methods are most evident when material costs are a high proportion of total costs, or average stocks are a high percentage of total assets, or there is a long production cycle. Unless selling prices in such conditions permit an acceptable margin above the current replacement cost of materials, the business concerned will find it hard to maintain its level of activity. This is why price quotations are so frequently made "subject to prices ruling at date of dispatch".

Like all profit-determination problems, the stock valuation problem comes back to this: which stock valuation system best matches current costs with current revenues? You in your timber yard have to ask yourself, as you sell a log, "What is the cost to me of this sale? The £5 I paid for it in period 1, or the £8 I must now pay to replace it?" You would be more realistic if you accepted that the sale has let you in for an expenditure of £8 on a replacement log (assuming you want to maintain your stock levels), than if you brought in an out-of-date cost of £5 and made plans to spend the £5 profit on something else. Your competitor may be delighted at his high profits during periods 2, 3, and 4, but if he spends this profit on a new piece of equipment he will not be able to spend it in replacing his stock of logs at the same rate as previously.

A business with a rapid turnover of stock, such as a super-market or a mail-order firm, will be less bothered with "cost of goods sold" problems than many industrial undertakings, and may well find cost-price relationships easier to control. Firms in which these problems are important are not, however, tied to either FIFO or LIFO; there are other methods, of which we shall briefly comment on two.

One way to avoid the FIFO/LIFO dilemma is to use the average cost method. The calculation is as shown in Table 15 for each item of stock.

TABLE 15

	Quantity	Unit cost	Value
		£	£
Opening stock	50	2	100
Purchases	20	2·7	54
Sub-total	70	2·2 (average)	154
Less Closing stock	30	2·2	66
Cost of goods sold	40	2·2	£88

To calculate average cost, add together the opening stock and purchases for the period and divide the money value with the quantity. Average cost will still lag behind current purchase prices, but to a less extent than FIFO. The time-lag will depend on the rate of stock-turn and the degree of price fluctuation. It is useful in situations where average prices are meaningful, i.e. where prices tend to fluctuate fairly evenly, and not too widely, round an average. You could quickly calculate your timber yard profits, based on average cost stock valuation, and compare the result with the profits shown in Table 15.

The second alternative to FIFO/LIFO is standard cost. This is not an actual cost at all, but an assumed cost. It may be the expected cost, or the hoped-for cost, or the target cost; the essential thing about it is that it is fixed in advance on the basis of all the factors affecting production during a given period, in so far as these are known or can be predicted. The standard cost of goods sold in a manufacturing concern will be the standard cost of materials, labour, and overheads, and in costing materials issued from the raw material stores to the shop floor, the use of a standard cost can avoid LIFO/FIFO problems, and also the clerical work of periodic averaging. Current price fluctuations have still to be taken into account, however, and this is usually done by comparing the invoiced price of goods received with the standard price. Losses and gains on standard prices are accumulated during the period and treated as an adjustment to either cost of goods sold or manufacturing overhead; losses on purchase are added, gains are subtracted. Compare Table 16 with Table 15.

TABLE 16

	Quantity	Standard cost	Standard value
		£	£
Opening stock	50	2·2	110
Purchases (at £2·7 each)	20	2·2	44
Sub-total	70		154
Less Closing stock	30	2·2	66
Standard cost of goods sold	40	2·2	88
Loss on purchase price (20 × £0·5)			10
Cost of goods sold			£98

We can now summarize the reported effect of purchase price changes under these four methods by comparing their effect on the data in Table 15.   Assuming that the opening stock of 50 units was purchased in the previous period at £2 per unit, the comparison is as shown in Table 17.

TABLE 17

	Quantity	Average cost	Standard cost	LIFO	FIFO
		£	£	£	£
Opening stock	50	100	110	100	100
Purchases	20	54	44	54	54
Sub-total	70	154	154	154	154
Less Closing stock	30	66	66	60	74
Standard cost of goods sold	—	—	88	—	—
Loss on purchase price	—	—	10	—	—
Cost of goods sold	40	£88	£98	£94	£80

The different methods of stock valuation can be compared by noting the different ways in which they apportion material purchase costs to past or future periods. LIFO values the expired benefits of delivered stock at the most recent purchase prices, while the unexpired benefit of stock on hand is valued at the oldest prices. FIFO does the opposite. Average price adds opening stock at previous average to purchases at historical cost, calculates a new average unit price, and applies it to both units released and units retained. Standard cost is like average price except that it attempts to predict a future average rather than accept an historical one. Standards and variances will be explained more fully in Chapter 8.

One other aspect of determining the cost of goods sold remains to be considered. This is a problem which arises in manufacturing firms, and comes about in this way. Suppose this time that you have a new product to market, and you have decided to set up your own plant and manufacture it yourself. The material in the product costs £12 and you pay a man £7 to produce one unit. There are also additional costs of £1 incurred in producing each unit, and this gives you a direct cost of £20 per unit. Manufacturing overheads are £6 per period, and selling and administration costs are £4 per period. Thus, your total costs in a period when you make one unit are £30. The finished product sells for £40. In period 1 you make one unit and sell none; in period 2 you make one and sell two. How do your profit and loss accounts look over these two periods? (Table 18).

TABLE 18. FULL COSTING
Profit and Loss Account

	Period 1	Period 2
Units manufactured:	1	1
Units sold:	0	2
	£	£
Opening stock	0	26
Direct cost	20	20
Manufacturing overhead	6	6
Total cost of finished goods	26	52
Less Closing stock	26	0
Cost of goods sold	0	52
Less Selling and administration	4	4
Total operating cost	4	56
Sales	0	80
Profit/loss[a]	£4[a]	£24
Profit per unit	—	12

These figures bring out several points. First, although you incurred expenditure of £30 in period 1 when there were no sales, you did not make a loss of £30, but only of £4; secondly, you carried over £26 of expenditure from period 1 to period 2 in the form of stocks; third, that by selling 2 units in period 2, you appear to have made a profit of £12 on each. But do you in fact make a profit of £12 per unit? Your original figures seemed to indicate that the profit would be £10 per unit.

What has happened is that by charging fixed manufacturing overhead to a unit of production, you have transferred its effect from the period when it was produced to the period when it was sold; assuming, that is, that the unit was in stock between the two periods. Is this logical? Should not fixed manufacturing costs (rent, insurances, etc.) be written off during the period of time they benefit, whatever the level of production, stocks, and sales? This is, after all, the way we treated selling and administration costs. The illustration above is based on the total costing, or full costing, approach. An alternative approach, known as direct costing, would give you a different answer. Under direct costing, only direct costs, i.e. those manufacturing costs which vary directly with the number of units produced, are charged into stock. Fixed manufacturing overheads are written off in the period in which they are incurred. The result is shown in Table 19.

The period 1 loss of £10 in Table 19 shows how overhead costs affect profits or losses more quickly with direct costing than with full costing. In periods when production activity is greater than sales activity (i.e. when stocks are increasing) direct costing produces a lower profit than full costing. When sales are higher than production (i.e. when stocks are decreasing) direct costing produces a higher profit than full costing. This is because goods are withdrawn from stock without the "stored" overhead costs which full costing would have apportioned to them. If production and sales are in balance and stocks are constant, direct and full costing will indicate the same profit figure.

The other thing to notice is the difference in profit per unit in period 2. Is not there a system which will give us the true profit of £10 per unit? The answer is, certainly. *Both* systems do—if you take a long enough period of time to eliminate the effects of stock fluctuations. Both illustrations begin and end with zero stocks, and both systems show a total profit for periods 1 and 2 of £20, which is £10 per unit in respect of the two units made

TABLE 19. DIRECT COSTING

Profit and Loss Account

	Period 1	Period 2
Units manufactured:	1	1
Units sold:	0	2
Opening stock	0	20
Materials and wages	20	20
Direct cost of finished goods	20	40
Less Closing stock	20	0
Cost of goods sold	0	40
Fixed manufacturing overhead	6	6
Selling and administration	4	4
Total operating cost	10	50
Sales	0	80
Profit/loss[a]	£10[a]	£30
Profit per unit	–	15

and sold in that time. Further ramifications of full and direct costing are covered in Chapters 7 and 8.

An exact correspondence between production volume and sales volume in a given period of time is not a feasible target for most businesses, and few businesses can solve the problem by carrying no stocks at all. Most businesses value their stocks for balance-sheet purposes at full manufacturing cost; use of the direct cost is thought to understate the value of the investment which the company has in its stocks. Supporters of direct cost argue that full costing tends to hide period costs away in stock values, and hence to mislead management on the amount of profit that has been realized during the period. Whatever system is chosen, it is important for a company to be consistent in the method used, and it is standard practice for any change in the basis of stock valuation to be clearly reported in the annual accounts.

The story is told of a managing director who, knowing that the previous month's sales were up, was eagerly awaiting the operating statement to see how well the company had done. To his amazement, when the operating statement arrived, it showed a loss of about £2500. The managing director queried the figures straightaway, certain that there had been a mistake. (Remember what we said in Chapter 1 about attacking the control system?) The chief accountant's explanation was very simple. Sales had indeed risen by £18,000, but production had been very low. The company operated a standard full costing system whereby fixed manufacturing overhead was charged to production at a standard rate per unit. When production fell below the level needed to absorb all the overhead, the amount of overhead carried into stock was less than the total overhead incurred, and the difference between overhead absorbed into products and actual overhead was written off against current profits. During the month in question, the unabsorbed overhead had more than offset the extra profit.

The managing director was baffled by all this. It seemed common sense to him that higher sales should mean higher profits. So the chief accountant, who had been bothered by this problem for some time, had another go at the figures. This time he took only the direct cost of goods sold and added to this the actual factory overhead plus the selling and administration costs for the period; in this way he arrived at a profit twice the size of the previous loss. (His assumptions about direct cost of goods sold meant, of course, that he had to write down the value of stock as shown in the balance sheet to exclude the fixed overhead content now dealt with directly. The fixed overhead deducted from the value of the opening stock had to be written off in the previous month, where it turned that month's profit into a loss.)

When the managing director saw the profit figure he was naturally delighted. But then he hesitated. "Does this mean more taxes?", he asked, "and more wage demands?" How would you answer this question?

The story highlights the problems that arise in income measurement because of the way in which the life of a business is broken down into financial years and regular accounting periods. A balance-sheet date arrives willy-nilly, regardless of whether or not it finds the business in a typical financial position or separates the spending part of a product cycle from its income-earning part. Accounting periods are arbitrary, but essential. So far no one has found a way of doing without them.

It is not the purpose of the story or of this chapter to show that profit is a meaningless figure drawn up to support a whim. This is very far from being the case. But it is true that a profit calculation can be based on different assumptions, assumptions mainly about which expenses properly belong in which period. People who are in business, whether to make or sell or add up the figures or supply the capital, would gain by understanding these assumptions. Unless the assumptions are understood and explained, they cannot be agreed or consistently applied to produce useful accounting information.

This chapter has been about profit. Profit is one of the necessary results of business operations, but it is not an ultimate goal in its own right. It is a means to an end, the "end" being to stay in business, survive its risks, and give satisfaction to all whom the business organization serves. "How much profit should we make?" is a question too often brushed aside with the over-simple answer "As much as possible, as quickly as possible". The chapter on budgets will return to this problem.

Some profit there must certainly be, and the marketing man is the one who secures it. Inside a business there are only cost centres; for profit you must go outside—to the market place.

Summary

The profit and loss account, or income statement, answers the question "How profitable were our sales in this period?" It reports the revenue realized by the business, which consists mainly of the invoiced value of goods dispatched or services rendered to customers during the period, but also includes other income from sidelines such as investments, rents, etc.

The profit and loss account then reports the expenses incurred in achieving realized revenue. The distinction between expenditure, expense, and payment is fundamental. Expenditure measures the cost of acquiring assets or services, expense measures in financial terms the extent to which those assets or services have been used up. Payment is the issue of cash or credit. In respect of the same business transaction, expenditure, expense, and payment may or may not coincide; they will often occur in different accounting periods.

In reporting the cost of goods sold, the profit and loss account will take in as much of the company's expenditure on purchase or manufacture of goods as can be attributed to goods dispatched during the period. Expenditure on goods held for dispatch in later periods is left in the balance sheet as an asset. The basis of the division of expenditure into expense and asset should be clearly understood by those who prepare and those who use profit and loss accounts, and should not be changed without good reasons clearly stated.

CHAPTER 4

A Closer Look
at Business Accounts

Now that we know something about the items to be found in balance sheets and profit and loss accounts, and understand how a financial measure can be put on these items, we can take a closer look at the relationships between these items. This chapter describes some of the ratios which businessmen apply to company accounts in order to get a better idea of the company's financial position and achievements, and, to some extent, of its prospects.

The essence of a ratio is the bringing together of two figures in order to compare them. This recalls what was said in Chapter 1 about the process of control, that it begins with comparison and leads when necessary to corrective action. One figure by itself is of no use. It must be compared with some other figure with which it has a relationship.

Balance-sheet ratios give an indication of a company's financial stability or strength, i.e. its ability at a point of time to meet and survive the claims made on it by those who finance it. Profit and loss account items can be used to calculate profitability ratios (i.e. ratios which indicate the return which operations during a period bring to invested funds) and turnover ratios (i.e. those which indicate the pace of operational activity). In taking this closer look at the finances of a business, it is essential to consider balance sheets and profit and loss accounts together. This is how company accounts are always prepared, since the two accounts are complementary. The business moves from a condition reported in balance sheet 1 to the condition reported in balance sheet 2,

TABLE 20. ANTONIO'S ICE-CREAM
Balance Sheet as at 31 October 19..

Sources	£	£	£	Assets	£	£	£
Ownership capital:				Goodwill, at cost			1000
Original capital	100						
Reserves	2204			Fixed assets, at cost:			
		2304		Land and buildings		4000	
Long-term liabilities:				Plant and machinery		400	
Mortgage (6% for 10 yr)	1000			Vehicles		1000	
Loan (6½% for 3 yr)	1900						5400
Future tax	1500			Current assets:			
		4400		Stock		180	
Current liabilities:				Debtors		670	
Bank overdraft	76			Cash		30	
Creditors	300						880
Accrued charges	50						
Proposed withdrawal of profit	150						
		576					
		£7280					£7280

TABLE 20 (CONT.)

Profit and Loss Account for 6 Months ending 31 October 19..

	£	£	£
Sales			6750
Cost of goods sold			2200
Gross profit			4550
Wages		180	
Overheads:			
Electricity	50		
Administration	150		
Distribution	271		
Loan interest	45		
		516	
			696
Operating profit (net profit before tax)			3854
Provision for tax			1500
Proposed withdrawal of profit			150
Net profit retained			2204
			£3854

mainly by the financial effects of its operations as reported in the profit and loss account.

Table 20 shows Antonio's balance sheet as at 31 October, and profit and loss account for the 6 months ending on that date are shown together. You might like to put a book-mark in this page, as we shall be turning back to these accounts from time to time.

Although many ratios are derived from figures taken from both accounts, it will be convenient to divide the description of ratios into two sections: balance-sheet ratios, and profitability and turnover ratios. To round off our examination of business accounts we shall consider a further accounting report which highlights the effect of recent operations on the movement of funds through the business; this is the funds flow statement.

Balance-sheet Ratios

Balance-sheet figures reflect a financial position at a given point of time, and the ratios derived from these figures give a guide to the stability of the business, i.e. its ability to meet the different claims made on it, both currently and in the longer term.

Many ratios can be calculated from balance-sheet figures alone, and we shall take three of these as being particularly relevant to marketing—the current ratio, the liquidity ratio, and the debt-ownership ratio.

Before calculating these ratios, it is useful to summarize a balance sheet under its main headings. Antonio's balance sheet on p. 27 could be summarized like Table 21.

The term "net worth" is customarily used to describe the total ownership stake in the business. Some people think that the net-worth figure ought to represent what the business would be worth to its owners if they put it up for sale. This is not so. The net worth means the amount of cash which the owners have put into the business plus any amounts due to them which have accumulated and been retained inside the business since it started. What a would-be purchaser would pay for the business is another matter. Net worth is to the value of the business what cost is to selling price. Since the term is a little misleading, we shall use the phrase "ownership capital" instead.

Intangibles are usually excluded from ratio calculations, simply because they are intangibles. If we did this, the summary would read as Table 22 shows.

The first ratio is the current ratio, in which total current assets are compared with total current liabilities. Current assets should normally be much greater than current liabilities, because they are the source from which current obligations are paid (suppliers, invoices, tax, etc.) and must necessarily be greater to provide a buffer against the uneven fluctuation of funds in and out of the business.

The difference between current assets and current liabilities is in fact the working capital of the business, which is why the

TABLE 21

Sources	£	%		Assets	£	%
Ownership capital (or "net worth")	2304	32		Intangibles	1000	14
Long-term liabilities	4400	60		Fixed assets	5400	74
Current liabilities	576	8		Current assets	880	12
	£7280	100			£7280	100

TABLE 22

Sources	£	%		Assets	£	%
Ownership capital (or "tangible net worth")	1304	21		Fixed assets	5400	86
Long-term liabilities	4400	70		Current assets	880	14
Current liabilities	576	9				
	£6280	100			£6280	100

current assets/ current liabilities ratio is also known as the working capital ratio. Working capital is the net amount of capital not tied up in fixed assets, but kept available to finance the circulation of current assets. The balance sheet (Table 3) on page 23 shows how Antonio divided his initial capital of £100 between fixed assets and working capital. We could summarize this balance sheet as Table 23 shows.

TABLE 23. ANTONIO'S ICE-CREAM
Balance Sheet as at 1 May 19..

Sources	£	Assets	£
Ownership capital	100	Fixed assets	82
		Working capital	18
	£100		£100

If Antonio had bought the machinery first, he would have been left with £18 in cash as his working capital. He uses this working capital to buy stock, some for cash, and some on credit. The working capital is his "float". Without it, there would be no current assets to circulate, no room for manœuvre in the variable ebb and flow of buying and selling.

A business could, of course, borrow its working capital, but this would make it vulnerable to extinction at the wish of a creditor. It is unusual for a well-run business to operate without working capital of its own.

When Antonio makes a profitable sale, his working capital increases. This is another reason why current assets should always exceed current liabilities. Operating profits are reflected in the current asset section of the balance sheet, at the point where stock becomes debtors. The excess of current assets over current liabilities will therefore increase with the inflow of profit, and will decrease with expenditure on anything but a current asset (i.e. on fixed assets or expenses), with losses and with withdrawals of capital. A business is heading for difficulty if expenditure on fixed assets and operating expenses reduces working capital more quickly than profit increases it.

A current ratio of 2:1 is often quoted as normal, but this may vary in different lines of business. Antonio's current ratio in the example above is £880 to £576, or 1·5:1. But remember that one of his current liabilities arose from his intention to draw out profit for a cruise; this is a liability of quite a different order from the liability to his suppliers. If Antonio put off his cruise for a year and left the £150 as retained earnings, his current ratio would become £880 to £426, or 2·1:1. In any case, these are early days for the business, which seems to be making a very promising start. Published accounts and the ratios drawn from them are not, however, designed to record future events, no matter how likely they may appear.

The acid test of liquidity (i.e. the ability to pay immediate debts) is shown by the liquidity ratio in which only current liquid assets are compared with current liabilities. Cash is, of course, the most liquid of all assets; debtors, too, are considered liquid, since they will provide cash within a short space of time. Investments which could be cashed at short notice would also count as liquid. The current asset which cannot normally be considered liquid is stock. A businessman selling on credit must first turn his stock into debtors before it will bring cash back into the business. The liquidity ratio therefore compares only debtors and cash (plus any readily marketable securities) with current liabilities. A 1:1 relationship is normally satisfactory; a lower ratio than this makes a business vulnerable to pressing demands from creditors. The firm's debt collection record is also relevant here, since quicker receipt of money from debtors obviously improves liquidity, though it will have no effect on the current ratio. Too high a level of stock may mean poor liquidity despite a satisfactory current ratio. And a businessman with over-high stocks is likely to be a poor sales prospect, as well as a greater credit risk.

In our example, Antonio has kept his stocks to only 20% of total current assets; cash and debtors are £700, against current liabilities of £576, a ratio of 1·2:1. To find out his debt collection record we need to know his *credit* sales for the period. These came to £3680, the rest of his sales being for cash. Average daily credit sales for the period were therefore £20 (3680 ÷ 184 days), so he will take about 33 days (670 ÷ 20) to collect the £670 worth of debtors on his books at 31 October. Whether this ought to be improved or not depends on the acceptable paying habits of the trading community in which Antonio operates. But remember that averages of this kind tend to imply that the rate of credit sale was fairly constant throughout the period whereas, during Antonio's first 6 months, this was almost certainly not the case.

Marketing people should remember the importance of liquidity, particularly in industrial selling or selling to retailers. No go-ahead industrial firm or village shop will buy goods that lie too long in stock. Hence the cartons labelled "Display to sell" or "Make your job easier by selling our products". Hence the point-of-sale gimmicks for the retailer. The aim is always the same: to keep stocks moving quickly through the business, so increasing profit, working capital, and liquidity. In this context, the salesman hopes to convince the buyer that he is speeding up the pace of the buyer's trading cycle, while the buyer keeps a sharp look out for products that might slow it down.

Firms buying and selling on credit (and what firm does not?) need particularly to watch liquidity. "Negative" liquidity arises when cash and debtors amount to less than current liabilities, and always needs to be watched. Inadequate liquidity may arise through either too slow or too fast a circulation of current assets. If the circulation is too slow, "negative liquidity" may arise, i.e. a situation in which liquid assets are less than current liabilities. One way of controlling this situation is to ask, "How much of my stock would I have to sell (at no more than the price I paid for it) in order to meet all current debts?" The answer will provide a percentage ratio which could be watched from month to month to see whether the position were improving or worsening. Table 24 illustrates the calculations required.

The management of Q Ltd., finding the company's liquidity strained at the end of January, would need to "cash" $7\frac{1}{2}\%$ of its stock if it had then to meet all current obligations. The position worsens during February, and the management determines to do

TABLE 24. Q LTD.

Liquidity Control Statement

	31 Jan.	28 Feb.	31 March
	£	£	£
Cash and debtors	12,000	12,500	19,500
Current liabilities	15,000	17,500	18,000
Deficiency of liquid assets	3,000	5,000	1,500
Stocks	40,000	50,000	30,000
% of stock value equal to liquid deficiency	7½%	10%	5%

something about it. Stock is reduced (purchases are cut, or sales are increased, or both) and cash and debtors are built up. As a result, the proportion of stock which would have to be realized to meet current liabilities falls to 5% at the end of March.

Note in passing that the liquidity information shown in Table 24 would be produced only while the liquid position is unsatisfactory. Control information is needed only in situations which are likely to call for corrective action, and should not be prepared and supplied once the corrective action has taken effect. Note also that taking corrective action on poor liquidity is not a good way to run a business; cash budgeting (see Chapter 6) should enable management to predict and control liquidity and prevent an undesirable strain on cash from arising. A final point for the marketing man to note: too many orders can be an embarrassment to a manufacturing firm when its liquidity is stretched, since production expenses are a drain on cash that will be needed, in due time, for the suppliers of goods already received, i.e. the creditors. On the other hand, a wholesaling or retailing firm with goods available for immediate transfer to customers might well ask its sales force to relieve liquidity precisely by getting more orders. The problem of balancing the level of sales with the level of financial resources can be a tricky one, and it will be considered in more detail in the chapter on current budgets.

Liquidity can also drop through too rapid a circulation of current assets. We noted above that expenditure on fixed assets and running expenses reduces working capital, and it is this sort of expenditure that an expanding business needs to incur. If the expansion also involves a build-up of stock to keep it in line with sales, conditions are ripe for over-trading. However, this situation can be more fully analysed by relating it to turnover, so we shall leave further discussion of over-trading till later in the chapter.

How should a business deal with a customer who is hard pressed to pay his account? It is quite easy to squeeze him for payment, and most sales ledger departments have a procedure for this; maybe a clerk is briefed to attach stickers to the month-end statements, each sticker more strongly worded than the last. The final missive may hint that a solicitor will intervene. Then the firm may forego direct action and hand the matter over to a debt collection agency. But a firm that really wants to sell will do better than this. It will recognize that a bankrupt customer is one customer less, and will look for ways of helping. The customer may have cut back on purchasing, but is unlikely to have stopped buying altogether. Probably he is making small cash purchases elsewhere, too embarrassed to get them from his main creditor. The creditor can at least go for the cash business, and so build goodwill for the future.

We have looked at liquidity in some detail because it indicates the ability of a business to meet its current financial obligations. To have a long-term future, a firm must obviously survive the immediate future. But the long-term prospect is also important, and likely financial strength and stability in the longer term, sometimes called solvency, can be tested by applying the debt–ownership ratio.

We saw that the sources of finance used in a business were of three main kinds: ownership capital, long-term liabilities, and current liabilities. The relationship between these three is something to watch. In Antonio's business the sources (shown in Table 22) are 21% ownership capital, 70% long-term debt, and 9% current debt.

Debt capital, or "loan capital", is a more risky source than ownership capital. Ownership capital will never have to be paid out while the business is running, but long-term debts will eventually have to be repaid, and cash will have to be available to meet these repayments when they fall due. If debenture holders or other suppliers of loan capital are not repaid promptly, they can take legal action to enforce payment, and in an extreme case could bring the debtor firm to bankruptcy. Furthermore, a business financed largely from borrowings is obliged to meet interest payments, whether it is doing well or not. Dividends on ownership capital, on the other hand, are payable only at the discretion of the directors; even a preference dividend may be deferred if the directors think the profits in a particular year are too low for a distribution.

Small businesses tend to be ownership financed, typically from private sources. Large companies more often than not show some form of loan capital in their balance sheets. All businesses will have current obligations. How much total debt should a business carry? Most businessmen in the normal course of industry and trade would probably prefer the ownership stake to be bigger than the non-ownership stake. No doubt Antonio looks forward to being in this position. At the moment his debt sources are 79% of total sources. To express this as a debt–ownership ratio, we would compare his total liabilities (£4976—see Table 22) with his own tangible stake in the business (£1304), and quote a ratio of 3·8:1. This may not look too good, but remember that Antonio is doing well and growing fast. His own stake has to increase only by £3672 to give a 1:1 debt–ownership ratio. How soon is this likely to happen if he maintains his present rate of growth and takes no more cruises? You should be able to work this out from Table 20 before you look at the footnote.*

---

* Table 20 shows that Antonio ploughed back £2204 during his first 6 months. At this rate, and with no further distributions of profit, he could retain £2354 every 6 months. He is therefore adding £2354 ÷ 6 = £392 per month to his own share in the business, and would take £3672 ÷ 392 = 9·35 months to bring his own stake up to the level of his borrowings.

The debt-ownership ratio is sometimes called the debt-equity ratio, or the ratio of total liabilities to tangible net worth.

A low debt–ownership ratio, indicating a high equity shareholding in a limited company, is a safe but challenging state of affairs. Safe because the firm is less vulnerable to pressure from long-term creditors, challenging because the equity shareholders, now the predominant source of finance, will rightly expect a bigger return on their investment than the company would guarantee to preference shareholders or debenture holders.

"Rarely, if ever", says an American authority on financial analysis, "should total liabilities of a commercial or industrial concern exceed the tangible net worth."* The main reasons for this are (a) creditors have more at stake in the business than the owners, (b) higher interest charges put up costs, possibly above the costs of competitors who are mainly owner financed, and (c) management may become less venturesome, preferring a secure if modest return to larger but more risky rewards. These reasons carry less weight when the company is doing well, but a high proportion of loan finance will aggravate the difficulties of a market recession. In such a situation, the predominantly loan-financed company will feel that it is battling away on behalf of the money-lenders rather than the owners. And when the sales manager of such a company tries to persuade the board to try new products and new markets, the board, with a cautious eye on high loan interest charges, may well say no.

In practice, few industrial companies ever settle into the position of being mainly loan-financed. High rates of tax, however, confer a significant advantage on the loan-financed company, because the interest charges reduce the amount of taxable profit. Nowadays, the company that issues £1000 in 6% debentures rather than £1000 of 6% preference shares will save itself tax on the £60 annual interest charge. With corporation tax at 40%, the additional cash retention by the company is £24 per annum.

The incidence of fixed interest claims focuses attention on

* Foulke, Roy A., *Practical Financial Statement Analysis*, McGraw-Hill, New York, 1961.

another ratio which is linked with the one we have just been considering; this is the capital gearing ratio. Capital gearing takes into account all long-term finance, whether loans or ownership investment, and compares the total fixed return portion (preference shares and loans) with the "discretionary return" portion (the ordinary shareholding).

Antonio's capital gearing and annual fixed interest charges are as Table 25 shows.

TABLE 25

Source of capital		Gearing	Annual fixed interest charges
	£	%	£
Ownership capital	100	3	—
Fixed interest sources	2900	97	184
	£3000	100%	

His gearing is extremely high, but will fall as he pays off the loans.

High gearing, then, describes a company with a high proportion of fixed dividend or interest capital. Capital gearing should be related to the degree of risk inherent in the company's ability to make profits; high gearing is generally appropriate for a fairly steady line of business in which profits will be moderate but regular and reliable; a business in unpredictable markets, or uncertain of much success at all (like gold-mining), would do better to remain low-geared. When profits fluctuate, high gearing can have a startling effect on the dividends paid to ordinary shareholders, as Table 26 shows.

The ordinary dividend in the low-geared company moves from 16% in year 1 to 6% in year 2, but in the high-geared company, the movement is from 96% in year 1 to only 4% in year 2.

In comparing debt capital with ownership capital, or fixed return sources with ordinary shareholdings, it has perhaps been

TABLE 26

Type of company	Year 1: high profits		Year 2: low profits	
	Dividend		Dividend	
	£	%	£	%
Low-geared company:				
Ordinary shares, £90,000	14,400	16	5,400	6
6% pref. shares, £10,000	600	6	600	6
Total dividend to be paid	£ 15,000		£6,000	
High-geared company:				
Ordinary shares, £10,000	9,600	96	400	4
6% pref. shares, £90,000	5,400	6	5,400	6
Total dividend to be paid	£15,000		£6,000	

implied that a high proportion of fixed return financing is undesirable. This is not necessarily so; it is all a question of risk. A
company with a significant percentage of fixed interest sources
can "trade on the equity", that is, use the lower-cost capital to
make high profits for the equity shareholders. Successful trading
on the equity does, however, call for consistently effective marketing, and while the rewards are great in good times, the draught
is felt more quickly in bad times. Trading on the equity is therefore something of an economic gamble, in which planned and
systematic marketing is the best way to reduce the risks.

Profitability and Turnover Ratios

Profitability ratios highlight and analyse the average amount of
profit per unit of sale during the period. Turnover ratios consider
the total amount of annual sales and relate this to the size of
the undertaking, measured in terms of the capital employed in it

and the value of the different assets under the control of the management.

These ratios are derived from three essential figures: assets, sales, profit. These three figures sum up the whole business process: assets are used to generate sales, which bring profit, or income, back to the enterprise. Assets and profit can have many meanings, so before we apply the ratios we must define our terms.

We shall take assets to mean total assets employed (the figure appearing at the bottom right hand of a traditional balance sheet set out as in Table 20), since the challenge to management is to use all its resources well, from whatever sources they are financed. The relevant profit figure here is net profit before tax, which represents the operating profit achieved by management. Tax laws obviously govern what part of this profit will remain with the shareholders, but that is a question for investors rather than for marketing people, whose financial problems lie in the hurly-burly of daily operations.

The overall measure of financial success in business is the ratio of *profit to assets*. Growth of total assets is not in itself a sign of success—any man with £5 in his pocket can treble his total assets by taking delivery of goods worth £10. Nor does an absolute figure of profit mean much by itself. We have to combine the two to show the measure of financial achievement.

The next question is, "How much selling did we have to do to bring in this profit?" Again, the absolute profit figure can look very different when placed alongside the value of sales needed to generate it. Our second basic ratio is therefore *profit to sales*, which measures the amount of profit earned per unit of sale, in this case the sales £.

Business assets are bought and used for the purpose of generating sales. How much sales revenue should the assets generate in a given period of time? How much sales can they generate, without deteriorating? Questions like these can be put into a quantitative form by using the next ratio, the ratio of *sales to assets*. This ratio measures asset turnover, i.e. the number of times in which each £ of assets has generated £1 worth of sales during the period. It is thus a measure of the speed of sales generation.

Antonio's ratios for his first 6 months in business are as follows:

$$\frac{\text{Profit}}{\text{Assets}} = \frac{£3854}{£7280} \times 100 = 53\%,$$

$$\frac{\text{Profit}}{\text{Sales}} = \frac{£3854}{£6750} \times 100 = 57\%,$$

$$\frac{\text{Sales}}{\text{Assets}} = \frac{£6750}{£7280} \times 100 = 93\% \text{ or } 0\cdot93 \text{ times.}$$

We will leave Antonio to decide whether or not these are the ratios which ought to have been achieved.

Some simple arithmetic will show that these three ratios are closely linked. The first one is the product of the other two:

$$\frac{\text{Profit}}{\text{Assets}} = \frac{\text{Profit}}{\text{Sales}} \times \frac{\text{Sales}}{\text{Assets}}$$

$$(53\% = 57\% \times 93\%).$$

To achieve a given profit to assets ratio, a business can operate with a high profit to sales ratio and a low sales to assets ratio, or vice versa. If assets are £100,000, and a profit of 25% on assets is required, this could be done either with a high volume of sales and a low profit on each sale, or with a smaller volume of sales and a higher profit on each £ of sales:

$$(a) \quad \frac{(\text{Profit}) \ £25,000}{(\text{Assets}) £100,000} = \frac{(\text{Profit}) \ £25,000}{(\text{Sales}) \ £500,000} \times \frac{(\text{Sales}) \ £500,000}{(\text{Assets}) £100,000}$$

or

$$(b) \quad \frac{(\text{Profit}) \ £25,000}{(\text{Assets}) £100,000} = \frac{(\text{Profit}) \ £25,000}{(\text{Sales}) \ £50,000} \times \frac{(\text{Sales}) \ £50,000}{(\text{Assets}) £100,000}$$

The data above would be expressed as ratios like this:

	Profit/Assets ratio		Profit/Sales ratio		Sales/Assets ratio
(a)	25%	=	5%	×	500% or 5 times
(b)	25%	=	50%	×	50% or 0·5 times

The relationship between sales volume and percentage profit per unit of sale will be very different in different lines of business. Compare, for example, a supermarket and a heavy engineering firm, each with total assets of £100,000, and each requiring 25% profit on assets. The supermarket can afford a low percentage margin on each £1 of sales, because it will effect £1 of sales very frequently. The engineering firm will require a high percentage margin on each £1 of sales, because it will effect £1 of sales less frequently than the supermarket.

The achievement of a profit appropriate to the size of the assets employed will therefore depend on achieving a balance between the profit to sales and the sales to assets ratios. This balance has to be consciously arrived at, and the actual ratios watched. A business in which the sales rose quickly and dramatically beyond the capacity of the assets is heading for danger, no matter how great the theoretical pile-up of profits.

It is not the philosophy of this book to encourage marketing people to go slow on getting orders. But an expanding order book is not enough in itself; it must be backed up with expanding purchasing, manufacturing, warehousing, delivery, and administrative facilities as well, assuming that spare capacity has already been taken up; and this means expanding the investment. This added investment has to be paid for, and we can now see how the higher return required on the higher investment can come from one or both of two sources: a greater volume of sales, and greater profit per sales £. The more profit a company can earn per sales £, the fewer sales £'s it has to chase after, and the greater the turnover capacity it still has up its sleeve.

We can use further ratios to analyse profitability. Profit is the residue between cost and revenue. If we analyse the costs into the main areas where they are incurred, we can ask whether the benefits flow in proportion to the cost.

This means a breakdown of the profit to sales ratio, based on an analysis of the sales £. This can be derived from the profit and loss account (Table 27).

The profit to sales ratio of 22·5% results from the other three

TABLE 27. COMPANY X

Profit and Loss Account: Year 1

	£	%
Production (=cost of goods sold)	47,800	59·2
Selling and distribution	6,200	7·7
General administration	8,500	10·6
Total operating costs	62,500	77·5
Operating profit	18,100	22·5
Sales	£80,600	100·0

operating cost ratios in which production costs, selling and distribution costs, and general administration costs are each expressed as a percentage of sales. Other departmental costs can be included if they are significant, e.g. research and development, engineering. This analysis summarizes the departmental consumption of revenue. The resulting ratios can be compared with similar ratios for previous periods or for other firms in the same line of business.

The asset turnover ratio can also be further analysed. This is done by analysing the composition of the assets. The right-hand-side of Company X's balance sheet reads as shown in Table 28.

TABLE 28

Assets	£	% of total assets	£	% of total assets
Fixed assets			29,000	67·5
Current assets:				
Stock	3500	8·1		
Debtors	9500	22·1		
Cash	1000	2·3		
Total current assets			14,000	32·5
Total assets			43,000	100·0

The first thing to watch is the proportion of fixed to current assets. The lower the proportion of current assets, the faster they have to circulate in order to generate a given turnover. The ratios of sales (S) to current assets (CA) (Table 29) show the different rates of generation for higher and lower current asset levels, assuming annual sales of £80,600 in each case:

TABLE 29.

(a) Current assets £14,000	(b) Current assets £20,000
$\dfrac{S}{CA} = \dfrac{80,600}{14,000}$	$\dfrac{S}{CA} = \dfrac{80,600}{20,000}$
= 5·7 times	= 4·0 times

But here it is not simply a question of choosing whether to have high current assets and slower turnover, or low current assets and a faster turnover. As we have seen, a sluggish turnover of current assets is the last thing any business wants. If current asset turnover is slowing down, or is slower than it should be, there are two main places where such assets can be tied up: stock and debtors. We can therefore use two further ratios to check where action is needed: sales to stock and credit sales to debtors.

Stock turnover is always an important thing to watch, since one of the major risks of business is that stocks may not be sold. The ratio of sales to stock shows how many times the sales revenue has absorbed the value of stock on hand, and is a rough guide to stock turnover. A better guide is to use the cost of goods sold, which will normally be a lower ratio than sales to stock. Cost of goods sold can be used to indicate physical stockturn, and also to calculate the average number of days for which stock has been held (Table 30).

TABLE 30. COMPANY X

Stock Turnover Ratios: Year 1

(a) $\dfrac{\text{Sales}}{\text{Stock}}$ $= \dfrac{£80,600}{£3,500} = 23$ times.

(b) $\dfrac{\text{Cost of goods sold}}{\text{Stock}}$ $= \dfrac{£47,800}{£3,500} = 13\cdot6$ times.

(c) Average days in stock $= \dfrac{£3,500}{£47,800} \times 365 = 27$ days

$(\dfrac{365}{13\cdot6} = 27$ days$)$.

The period-end stock figure may not be representative of average stock levels throughout the year, and if there has been unusual stock movement around balance-sheet date, an average stock figure would give a more meaningful comparison. The average could be the mean of opening stock and closing stock for the year, or of the month-end stocks during the year.

The other possible "resting place" for slow-moving current assets is debtors. Debtors, too, can be expressed either as a turnover ratio or as a "number of days" figure, i.e. the average collection period. We referred to this earlier in connection with liquidity. Most industrial firms sell entirely on credit, but some have mixed wholesale and retail outlets. Before calculating an average collection period, it is worth making sure that the sales figure used refers only to *credit* sales, or the result of the calculation will not be meaningful or useful. Assuming that Company X sells only on credit, the average collection period it allows from its debtors is:

$$\frac{\text{Debtors}}{\text{Annual credit sales}} \times 365$$

$$= \frac{£9,500}{£80,600} \times 365 = 35 \text{ days}.$$

Similarly, the payment period for settling creditors' accounts can be calculated, using creditors as the numerator and annual credit purchases as the denominator.

The scheme of ratios described above is summarized in Table 31. It would be tempting to close off the asset turnover ratios by comparing cash in hand with sales; cash is the only asset left out. This would, however, be absurd. The level of cash in a business at balance-sheet date has no meaning in relation to sales; it has no meaning in relation to anything except the company's need or wish to spend it. These things are taken care of by the current and liquidity ratios, which we have already dealt with, and by cash budgeting, which we shall cover in Chapter 6.

Ratios are useful indicators of trends in the way in which the business is using the funds committed to it, but the precision of the ratios themselves, often worked out to decimal points, should not blind us to their limitations. Ratios are merely arithmetic derivations, and take no note of the changing conditions in which a firm will find itself from year to year. Comparison of one firm's ratios with those of other firms will be of limited value if accounting conventions in each firm are not consistently applied. Official inter-firm comparisons (such as those arranged by trade associations or the Centre for Interfirm Comparison Ltd.) make every effort to ensure comparability, but people making unofficial or broader comparisons will not have the same opportunity to do this. For example, "The Times 300", published annually in *The Times Review of Industry and Technology*, lists in order of size the 300 largest industrial companies in Britain, size being measured by the capital employed as reported by each company. Capital employed is defined as "total tangible assets less current liabilities and sundry provisions (excluding bank loans and overdrafts and future tax)". There might well be some changes in this "league table" if all companies adopted exactly the same method of valuing their assets, sources, and expenses. Such absolute consistency is neither necessary nor desirable; figures in business are a means, not an end. "The Times 300" is offered as a descriptive guide, and includes a warning against unjustified inferences which all users of financial information could bear in mind: "It is clear that in some instances crude calculations from which morals were drawn would be misleading."

TABLE 31. SUMMARY OF RATIOS

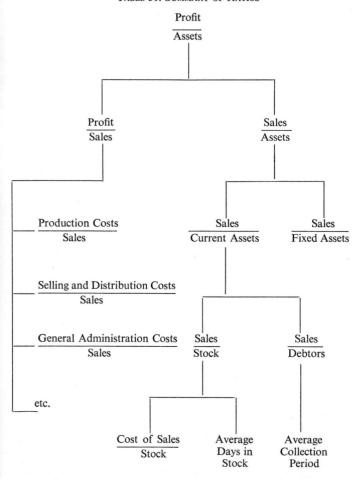

Another characteristic of ratios is that they cover events with a blanket of averages which may easily mislead. We noted the overall sales to debtors ratio as one instance of this. The fact that Antonio's business became a mixture of manufacturing, whole-saling, and retailing made it less suitable for ratio-based inferences, which is why we switched to Company X for the analysis of profitability and asset turnover ratios.

Nevertheless, the information that we have is meaningful and useful to the extent that the contents of Chapters 2, 3, and 4 have been understood, and we are far better off with it than without it. It will not, of course, solve our business problems; ratio analysis is a device, not for giving answers, but for suggesting questions which need answers. The fundamental question comes to this: "Are these ratios satisfactory in the circumstances, and are they moving the way we want them to?"

How do ratios move? They move as business events move, and some measure of this movement can be gained by comparing the ratios for one set of company accounts with similar ratios derived from the accounts of the previous year. Early in Chapter 2 we said that company accounts always show the previous year's balance-sheet figures alongside the newly reported figures, thus revealing the changes in financial structure that have occurred between the two balance-sheet dates. Much of the significance of these changes will be lost unless we do some homework on the figures. This can be done first by compiling and comparing parallel sets of ratios, and, secondly, by preparing a funds flow statement.

Funds Flow Statements

A balance sheet summarizes the different categories of finance which have been put into and left in a business from the day it started (these are the sources), and also the assets which have been acquired since the business began and which still remain to be used up. Often the business has been going for a very long time, and many of the transactions recorded in the balance sheet are old history. People interested in the business are more concerned with the immediate past than with earlier financial history, and the funds-flow statement summarizes how funds, both long-term and short-term, have been obtained and used during the accounting period just ended.

The significance of such a statement is that it shows the results achieved by management during the past year in their efforts to control company finances, and in particular to secure a satisfactory inflow of funds from marketing operations. But it is not enough to watch the inflow of funds. How they are used is also of major interest, and in a company that wants to get somewhere, the balancing of long-term and short-term finances is a matter for continuous attention at all levels. The funds-flow statement will help to focus this attention.

Where in the accounts can we look to see this broad flow of funds? In the cash book? No; the cash transactions, even in monthly or yearly summary, reflect the complications of payment schedules and credit needs which are irrelevant to funds flow. Funds are financial values given and received, and financial values can change hands without any flow of cash, e.g. when goods are bought on credit. What about the profit and loss account, then? We know that profits do not represent cash. However, the profit and loss account is not the place either; for one thing, it contains no explicit reference to the flow of capital funds, and these are obviously important.

The place to look for the effect of funds flow is in the working capital accounts. All funds move through working capital, and a summary of the inputs and outputs to working capital will tell us what we are looking for. Working capital is the buffer between long-term and current finance; it is the shock absorber between the chassis (fixed assets) and the wheels (current assets); the size of it is crucial, but beyond saying that it should be neither too big nor too small, there are no rules of thumb to tell you exactly what it should be. Working capital is constantly changing because of the movement of funds from a source, through the working capital account, to an application or use. The changes can be summarized in the traditional stock account form:

Working capital at start of period
+ Transactions increasing working capital (sources of funds)
= Total working capital available during period

Less Transactions reducing working capital (application of funds)

= Working capital at end of period.

To illustrate funds flow, we can return to Antonio. It is now many years since he hung up his white coat on the door of his little headquarters in Margate. By shrewd marketing, a compelling ambition to lead the field, and by the skilful handling of a series of takeovers, Antonio has become the top man of a giant dairy empire, the British Dairy Corporation Limited. The most recent accounts of the corporation are printed as Table 32, and we can draw up a fund-flow statement from these accounts.

It is possible to get some inkling of funds flow by reducing the two balance sheets (this year's and last year's) to their main headings and setting them out in columnar form (Table 33).

TABLE 33. NATIONAL DAIRY CORPORATION LTD.

Group Balance Sheets as at 31 March

	This year	Last year	Difference (+ = increase − = decrease)
	£'000	£'000	£'000
1. Goodwill	19,408	18,020	+ 1388
2. Fixed assets	49,631	47,028	+ 2603
3. Investments	482	582	− 100
4. Total non-current assets (1 + 2 + 3)	69,521	65,630	+ 3891
5. Current assets	31,316	30,480	+ 836
6. *Less* Current liabilities	22,764	20,044	+ 2720
7. Net working capital (5–6)	8,552	10,436	− 1884
8. Net assets employed (4–7)	78,073	76,066	+ 2007
9. *Less* long-term liabilities	14,171	14,869	− 698
10. Ownership capital (8–9)	£63,902	£61,197	+ 2705

Iss
Ca
Re

To

Fu

Ou

Lo

Pr

Cu

This comparison can begin to hint at the flow of funds during the recent year. It shows, for example, that the investment in fixed assets has increased by £2,603,000; that current liabilities have gone up by £2,720,000, while current assets are up by only £836,000, making a decrease in net working capital of £1,884,000. But these broad hints are not sufficiently explicit about many of the key areas in which major decisions need to be taken. The growth in ownership capital is the net result of many successive decisions, decisions, for example, on what operating activity shall be carried out at what cost to realize the company's net income, how much of this income shall be applied to fixed assets and how much in dividends for shareholders, and so on. Funds-flow statements are intended to pin-point as far as possible the results of the major decisions on financial policy which were made, or should have been made, at the start of and during the period under review.

There are no general rules on what should go into a funds-flow statement, beyond the fact that the results of important financial decisions should be explicitly referred to. Figure 4 illustrates the main sources and uses of funds which are generally the subject of financial policy, and indicates that movement of funds is two-way; any or all of these categories can be either source or application, depending on whether the net effect is to reduce working capital or to increase it.

The diagram reminds us how a business works. Long-term, and usually irreversible decisions are made to raise capital from ownership or non-ownership sources and to invest it partly in fixed assets and partly in working capital. All this presupposes the biggest decision of all: what operations should the business engage in? This decision is essentially a marketing decision, and is again irreversible in the short-term, though it needs to be adapted and developed in the light of environmental opportunities. Working capital is used to set in motion the operating cycle in which decisions are short-term, but need to be taken in the light of long-term objectives and possibilities.

The diagram at Fig. 4 is designed to bring out the relationship

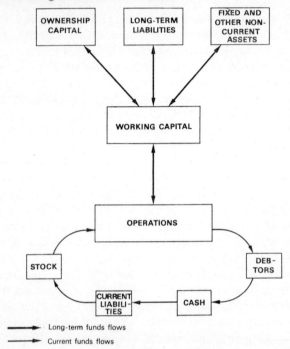

FIG. 4. Flow of funds through working capital.

between the longer term financial decisions and current financial decisions. Both sets of decisions depend for their implementation on an adequate supply of working capital.

Sources of funds are the areas from which funds have moved into working capital. Applications, or uses, of funds are the movement of funds out of working capital. If total sources exceed total applications, the resulting increase in working capital is itself an application of funds. If total applications exceed total sources, the resulting decrease in working capital is itself a source of funds.

The four major source and application areas are ownership capital, long-term liabilities, fixed and other non-current assets, and operations. In these areas, we shall want to know movements in both directions, if they have occurred. The published accounts may not always give us this information, and some estimating may have to be done. As far as current sources and applications are concerned, the detailed funds flows are so numerous and complex that all we need to watch in the funds-flow statement is the net increase or decrease over the year. How many specific areas are watched will depend on which ones are currently the subject of important decisions, but five areas are usually of interest in most businesses. Three areas emerge from a breakdown of current assets, (stock, debtors, cash) and two from a breakdown of current liabilities (creditors and other).

The exact format of a funds flow statement depends as always on the needs and convenience of the user. The layout adopted for the British Dairy Corporation Funds Flow Statement in Table 34 illustrates the explanation given above, and reveals as much as can be deduced from the published accounts. Access to the books of the Corporation would be needed to give the directors a more complete picture of the scope they had for redeploying their financial resources.

This particular funds flow presentation is in two parts: the sources and applications of funds, and an analysis of working capital changes in terms of current assets and liabilities. The items in the main part of the statement are matters for decisions affecting operations and finances in the longer term, and which are largely irreversible. Funds from operations are not entirely in this category, although they result in large measure from a long-term decision to operate in certain markets. But they also accumulate as a result of the skill of operating management in controlling current conditions in that market. To that extent, funds from operations also have a current aspect; they result from decisions made in the course of the cycle of operations, in which corrective action, involving the reversal or modification of previous decisions, can take effect much more quickly.

Many funds-flow statements omit reference to current sources and applications, but such reference should be included if it

TABLE 34. BRITISH DAIRY CORPORATION LTD. AND ITS SUBSIDIARIES

Funds Flow Statement, 19..

	£'000	£'000
Sources:		
Funds generated by operations	8642	
Proceeds on sale of non-current assets	157	
Funds received from mortgage repayments	106	
Increase in tax liability	56	
Increase in provisions	57	
Total sources	———	9,018
Applications:		
Dividends	2275	
Purchase of non-current assets (net)	7776	
Expenses on issue of bonus shares	40	
Acquisition of shares in subsidiary companies	156	
Partial transfer of pension liability	635	
Reduction of loan to overseas subsidiary	20	
Total applications	———	10,902
Net decrease in working capital		£1,884

Analysis of working capital changes:

	£'000	£'000
Current sources:		
Decrease in cash and short-term securities	2851	
Increase in creditors	1586	
Increase in bank overdraft	1121	
Net increase in other current liabilities	13	
Total current sources	———	5571
Current applications:		
Increase in stock	2303	
Increase in debtors	1384	
Total current applications	———	3687
Net decrease in working capital		£1884

reveals a state of affairs which needs watching. At present, funds-flow statements are seldom found in annual company accounts despite the fact that they contribute usefully to an understanding of the financial progress of the business.

It is not immediately obvious where the amounts shown in Table 34 came from, so a word of explanation about each will be helpful. All the figures relate to the balance-sheet changes previously noted, but by referring to the profit and loss account, and to other information in the notes to the accounts (not reproduced here), we can explain the balance-sheet changes more fully.

Funds generated by operations—£8,642,000

This is not the same as net profit, since operations generate more funds than the net profit figure indicates. Operations bring in current funds regardless of the loss of benefit from funds applied in previous years, i.e. regardless of depreciation charges. The funds generated by operations are the revenue from sales less "cash" expenses, i.e. expenses for which cash has been paid or will be paid at some future time—the timing does not matter.

Frequently, total sales revenue is not disclosed. In that case, funds from operations can be arrived at another way, by adding depreciation back to net profit, i.e. net profit after tax. (Tax is normally treated as an operating expense for funds-flow purposes, since it is an inflow of funds attributable to a creditor, the government, and not to the business.) Calculation of funds due to operations by adding back depreciation gives the same answer as the previous method, but tends to mislead people into thinking that depreciation is an additional source of funds. This is not so; the funds are brought in by the operations, not by the depreciation charge.

We shall have to use the latter method here, for lack of a turn-over figure. Funds from operations are £4,863,000 (profit attributable to British Dairy Corporation Ltd.) plus £3,779,000 (depreciation of fixed assets), which comes to £8,642,000.

Marketing people will not be slow to note that funds from operations, which means marketing operations, account for 97% of all funds coming in to the Corporation during the year. They must surely be at least curious as to what happens to these funds.

Proceeds on sale of non-current assets—£157,000

This figure was disclosed in the notes to the accounts and covers the profit on sale of fixed assets and investments. It is in fact a net figure, representing the proceeds of sale less the book value of fixed assets disposed of, which was probably not considerable. Profit on the sale of fixed assets or investments brings an increase in capital reserves, and this figure helps to explain the balance-sheet difference of £4,585,000 (£11,183,000 less £15,768,000) which will be fully explained later.

Funds received from mortgage repayments—£106,000

This is the balance-sheet difference between the figures shown last year and this year for mortgages on freehold properties. The Corporation has reduced the money it has out in mortgages by £106,000, but this may well be the net difference between amounts called in and new advances made. However, it is sufficient to report the net result of mortgage transactions, particularly since the amount is only $1 \cdot 2 \%$ of all long-term sources.

Increase in tax liability—£56,000

This results from calculations made by the Corporation's accountants and auditors, and it may be difficult to understand how a group of men discussing figures round a table can cause an outflow of funds. The answer is that they do not. The outflow of funds in this case is caused by tax legislation, and arises simultaneously with the inflow of taxable funds. For convenience, the extent of the outflow is measured only once a year.

Increase in provisions—£57,000

Provisions are amounts set aside to meet a known liability of unknown amount. The accounts give no hint as to the nature of these provisions, and the increase of £57,000 reflects the

Corporation's judgement of the extent to which these outside claims of unknown amount are likely to make increased calls on the funds invested in the Corporation.

Dividends—£2,275,000

This is the first application of funds listed, and is taken from the appropriation section of the profit and loss account.

Purchase of non-current assets (net)—£7,776,000

This figure has to be deduced, since no information is given about the total expenditure on fixed and other non-current assets, nor on the amount realized on the sale of fixed assets. We have dealt separately with the mortgage amounts (though these could have been included in this calculation), so the balance-sheet difference we have to explain relates only to goodwill, fixed assets, and trade investments. Last year these totalled £65,310,000; this year's figure was £69,307,000. The book value of these assets therefore increased by £3,997,000 during the year. But since fixed assets were depreciated by £3,779,000 during the year (see profit and loss account), it follows that total purchases were at least the sum of these two amounts, to bring non-current assets up to this year's book figure. The two amounts total £7,776,000, and while this is certainly an understatement, it is a better guide than the simple balance-sheet difference.

The total of £7,776,000 could be itemized if thought useful, by showing separately the increased investment in goodwill, fixed assets, and trade investments.

Expenses on issue of bonus shares—£40,000

This was given in the notes attached to the published accounts. We can now explain the difference of £117,000 between last year's share capital and capital reserves and this year's. The issued share capital rose by £4,702,000. As this was a bonus issue, brought about by the capitalization of capital reserves, funds flow was not affected. Capital reserves, however, fell by only £4,585,000, indicating an increase of £117,000 in capital reserves for some other reason. The increase was in fact the receipt of £157,000 "cash" profit (whether or not actually received during the year) on the sale of fixed assets and investments, less the £40,000 paid in issue expenses. Both these items are part of the funds flow.

Acquisition of shares in subsidiary companies—£156,000

This is the drop in minority shareholdings in subsidiaries which occurred between the two balance-sheet dates. Notes to the accounts explain that the Corporation has purchased preference shares in its subsidiaries to the value of £156,000.

Partial transfer of pension liability—£635,000

The pensions and superannuation provision has dropped by this amount during the year because the Corporation has handed over to an insurance company part of its liability to pay pensions and superannuation. This has cost £635,000.

Reduction of loan to overseas subsidiary—£20,000

This is the balance-sheet difference of £20,000 for the item "secured loan in overseas subsidiary".

Net decrease in working capital—£1,884,000

The sources and applications listed above result in a net decrease in working capital, which is the balancing source required to provide sufficient funds for all the applications. The accuracy of the calculations can be checked by comparing this amount with the movements in current assets and current liabilities during the year.

The detailed changes in current assets and current liabilities as reported in the lower part of the funds-flow statement correspond with the differences between these items in the two balance sheets. They summarize the financial results achieved by the operating management of the Corporation, results which can now be seen to be closely linked with the results of funds control at policy-making levels.

This concludes our description of the generally accepted techniques of company accounts analysis. Any reader who wants to see more clearly how the finances of the British Dairy Corporation are shaping can now apply ratios, ratio trends, and funds flow to help him find out. The balance sheets and income statements of the Corporation are more complex than the simple accounts which reflected Antonio's first business transactions, but they have the same basic structure, and lend themselves to the same kind of analysis.

Summary

Ratio analysis compares different components of company accounts—sources, assets, expenses, and revenue, and brings out significant relationships between these components. The main ratios offer a periodic check on (a) the relationship between the amount invested in a business and the return which business operations over a given period bring to that investment, and (b) the general soundness of the financial condition of the business, i.e. its ability to meet the financial claims made on it.

Ratios can be applied to a single set of company accounts, but are best seen in a series, to show the way in which financial relationships are moving. Judgements based on ratio analysis should take into account the financial conditions which are normal and acceptable in the type of business under consideration.

Funds flow indicates the main ways in which new funds coming into the business have been used. Chief among these sources of funds are the funds generated by marketing operations.

Whether or not the analysis of company accounts calls for control action depends on the extent to which reported events approach or coincide with planned events. For operating managers, techniques of financial analysis will be of most use when used predictively, i.e. in answer to the question "What kind of a financial return, what kind of a financial structure, do we want to bring about?" Questions of this kind make managers look ahead, and this brings us to budgets.

CHAPTER 5

Looking Ahead:
The Long-term Decisions

EVERYTHING we have said so far about business finance has been related to past events. But we cannot control the past no matter how much we analyse it. We can only plan to do better for the future. The process of control begins with an awareness of an objective to be reached at some time in the future. Marketing control, for example, is always looking to the future. It looks at future changes in customer needs, future ways of satisfying customers, future trends in marketing outlets, future advertising media, future marketing costs.

The main reason for analysing the past is to learn from it for the future. Company finances are usually analysed to provide some indication, however tentative, of the direction in which they are likely to move and of the action needed to ensure that progress is maintained. The need for corrective action is more readily appreciated if actual events are compared with the desired events outlined in a plan. Financial control, like marketing control, looks to the future and asks, "What financial results do we want? What will it cost us to carry out our plans? What sort of a financial position shall we be in, 3 months ahead, a year ahead?" Since the major determinant of financial strength is the profit generated by marketing operations, we shall not be surprised to find that marketing control and financial control are closely interlinked.

Financial control in a business usually involves the familiar process of budgeting, and that is what these next two chapters are about. At one extreme, budgets can be used to cramp initiative or encourage wasteful expenditure. Such activities are the result of poor management rather than of budgeting as such. The sort of budgets that are useful to a business are those which express plans in the common language of money, integrate departmental plans into a master plan for the whole company, and stand up to the kind of financial analysis described in the previous chapter. With budgets, however, values are attached to predicted rather than to past events. A final hallmark of useful budgets is that they are flexible, and allow scope for adjustment as experience confirms or modifies the budget assumptions.

A series of events has a beginning and an end. The events which make up a financial period in the life of a business also have a reported beginning and an end: the opening and closing balance sheets. These documents are convenient milestones with which to mark out progress. Imagine, then, the directors of Z Ltd., who are meeting to map out the company's future operations. They have before them a balance sheet as at the start of the budget period. This balance sheet will not be an actual balance sheet because they will be meeting a little before the end of the current period, but we can assume that they are near enough balance-sheet date to make a reasonably accurate prediction of what the financial position will be when they get there (Table 35).

This balance sheet is a jumping off ground, and the first question which must be decided is "How big a jump are we considering?" In accounting terms, this means deciding the length of the budget period.

The accounting year is firmly embedded in financial planning, and with good reasons, but it is not necessarily ideal for all budget purposes. Longer-term forecasts may be needed for 5 or 10 years ahead. On the other hand, quarterly or even monthly predictions will probably be more accurate. Some firms use "running" budgets in which broad yearly plans are made, but each quarter the plans are reviewed, the quarter just elapsed is discarded from the annual budget and another quarter, beginning in 9 months, is added.

Table 35. Z Ltd.
Balance Sheet as at 1 July 19..

Sources	£	£	Assets	£	£
Share capital		80,000	Fixed assets at cost	150,000	
Reserves		117,000	*Less* Depreciation to date	40,000	110,000
Current liabilities:			Current assets:		
Tax	22,000		Raw materials	14,000	
Creditors	36,000		Work-in-progress	40,000	
Total current liabilities		58,000	Finished goods	10,000	
			Total stock	64,000	
			Debtors	44,000	
			Cash, etc.	37,000	
			Total current assets		145,000
		£255,000			£255,000

There is another kind of budget period which to a large extent ignores the calendar and focuses attention on the life-cycle of a product. This division of time is in many ways more natural for a business than calendar periods, and is particularly useful because it links marketing, production, and financial planning into a unified whole, based on an acceptable rate of return on the capital invested. Planning of this kind, involving capital investment in a production and marketing project has techniques of its own which offer a useful guide to long-term decision making. The detailed operational planning to be described in Chapter 6 will be most effective when it is developed from the long-term plans. The assumption of this book is that long-term plans need to be carefully formulated and widely shared among the managers who will be expected to carry them out. Unless this is done, operating budgets will be unrealistic and field salesmen in particular may well find themselves with an impossible task.

It is fairly common practice nowadays for long-term investment proposals to be made to the board of directors by the executive heads of operating departments. This is usually a sign of healthy two-way communication between executives and policy-makers. However, the final decision is normally reserved to the board itself, because of the far-reaching effect of capital decisions and because, once embarked upon, such decisions are almost always irreversible.

In considering the next few months, the directors of Z Ltd. have to bear in mind a capital expenditure decision they made some time previously. The unusually high liquidity of the company (over 2:1) is not fortuitous; the directors have long-term plans for expansion and will shortly incur capital expenditure of some £25,000 on new plant and machinery. Months ago, when they looked at all the opportunities available to them, they were faced with the problem of choosing the most acceptable of various proposals put up for their consideration. How did they do this?

The first decisions they had to make were marketing decisions. What markets were they in? What markets did they want to enter?

What share of these markets could they get? What were their competitors doing? The purpose of business activity can never be adequately described solely in terms of making a profit. Business earnings are rewards for giving customer service, and fundamental questions at least as important as "How much profit?" are "How much service, and of what kind, and for how long?"

The decisions made on markets, market share, and product innovation define the limits of the next decision area: Do we make or buy the product? Product innovation normally implies product manufacture, so the next question is, What plant do we need, how much will it produce, and how long will it last? These can be tricky decisions, because of the need to balance the life of the machinery with the optimum market life of the product. It is wasteful to buy a machine to last for 50 years when the product it makes will not sell beyond 5. On the other hand, a machine that will just last for 5 years might well start to break down after only 4. And what chance is there of a better machine coming out in 3 years time?

These marketing and technical questions all have financial ramifications. The financial decisions come down to this: if there is a single capital expenditure proposal to consider, will the investment yield as good a return over the project life as the company gets at present on the capital it is using? The answer is either yes or no; go ahead or do not go ahead. But if there are several projects all competing for the same amount of capital, the question is, which of these proposals is most acceptable, i.e. which will bring the highest return?

In trying to predict the future return from a business project it is obvious that everything hangs on the reliability of the sales forecast. No forecast can be perfect, but this is no reason for not making as good an attempt as possible.

The remainder of this chapter describes different methods of evaluating the profitability of capital projects. But it must be stressed from the outset that financial considerations are not the only ones which weigh with a board of directors. Factors such as social responsibility, prestige, alleged improvement in efficiency, or other intangible reasons may well override the purely financial indications. It is as well, however, to be clear on what the financial considerations are.

The evaluation of capital projects forces the management of a business to compare two essentially unlike things: a large initial outlay of cash, on the one hand, and a return flow of smaller amounts of cash, spread over several years, on the other. But the comparison is simplified by reason of the fact that many of the problems of accounting measurement disappear, particularly those problems related to the allocation of costs to time periods, and the distinction between expenditures and expense. The reason for this is that in the course of a long-term project, all expenditures will be seen as expenses, and all claims relating to the project will be paid out in cash. The project will be considered in isolation and in its entirety; there will therefore be no need to disentangle capital from revenue expenditure, or allocate depreciation charges, or apportion overheads. All that matters is the additional cash flows in and out of the business which will take place as a result of the project, and which would not take place if the project were not undertaken.

Looked at like this, a direct investment in a business project is measured in just the same way as a purely financial investment. A bank making a loan will consider the amount of the loan, the length of time it is to run, and the appropriate rate of interest to be charged. It will control the loan, which is an investment, by ensuring that the amount to be lent is passed to the borrower at the agreed time, and that the borrower repays interest and capital at the due dates. The only difference with investment by the board in a business project is that there is no firm agreement between the company and the market as to what the return shall be. The company has to work for it, and can only put a percentage rate of return on it after it has been earned. But all the characteristics of financial investment are present in the project investment, namely (1) the outlay of a predetermined amount at an agreed time, (2) for an agreed period, with the expectation that (3) the project will yield a sufficient return to replace the capital sum intact plus (4) an amount equal to a reasonable rate of interest.

The directors of Z Ltd. will therefore need to develop some skill in predicting differential (or "incremental") cash flows. Paradoxically, this task can be more complex than it need be by reason of the fact that the accounting "if's and but's" of Chapters 2, 3, and 4 have largely to be ignored.

There are two main questions to be answered in predicting the cash flow for a project: first, what is the outlay? Secondly, what is the income?

The outlay will be mainly the purchase and installation costs of new plant. But there will also be initial revenue expenditure (an advertising campaign, perhaps, or recruiting, and training salesmen or factory personnel), and extra working capital needed to finance stocks and debtors pending the return of cash from customers.

The income will be the difference between the realized sales value of products sold and the cash outgoings necessary to achieve the sales. These outgoings will be the costs of all goods and services used in manufacturing and distributing the product, and also tax payments, which would not, of course, be incurred if the project were not undertaken. (The calculation of tax follows regulations laid down by the Inland Revenue, and need not concern us here. It should be mentioned that depreciation has to be brought into the calculation at this point because it is an allowable deduction from income which reduces the tax liability. However, the depreciation figure used is calculated in accordance with the tax regulations, and not necessarily by the same method as that used elsewhere in the company's books.) The income will thus be similar in nature to the "funds generated by operations" (less tax) which we considered towards the end of Chapter 4.

Alternatively, a capital project may be undertaken—not to make and sell a new product—but to improve the efficiency of working methods. The income from such projects takes the form of cash savings rather than cash profits. In both types of project the cash inflow in the final year of operation will include sums realized on the disposal of fixed assets and the release of working capital no longer needed in the project.

Once the appropriate amounts have been satisfactorily predicted, the cash flow can be summarized year by year for each year of the life of the project. The convention in cash-flow statements is to assume that all transactions occur on the final day of the year (some analysts make it the first day of each year), and to call the year of the initial outlay "year 0". Subsequent years will be numbered from 1 upwards. Capital outlay can, of course, continue during the years following year 0. Outflows of cash are negative flows, inflows are positive. For convenience a cash-flow calculation sheet could be set out as Table 36 shows, the net income (or "aggregate cash flow") for the whole project being the difference between total outflows and total inflows.

TABLE 36.
Project X: Cash Flow Calculation

Year	(1) Outflows (−) Fixed assets, initial revenue costs, working capital, cash operating costs	(2) Inflows (+) Sales revenue or cost savings, return of working capital, final sale of assets	(3) Net Cash Generation (− or +)
	£	£	£
0			
1			
2			
3			
4			
etc.			
Net income			

Inside Z Ltd. three proposals have been worked out as described above and submitted to the board. All three involve the launching of a new product. The pattern of expenditure and the response of the market is different in each case, although all projects have a life of 6 years. The figures of most interest to the directors are those giving the net cash generation, and for the three projects they are as Table 37 shows.

TABLE 37. Z LTD.

Net Cash Generation of Proposed Projects A, B, and C

Year	Project A	Project B	Project C
	£'000	£'000	£'000
0 (initial outlay)	− 25	− 30	− 25
1	+ 11	+ 4	+ 4
2	+ 10	+ 11	+ 4
3	+ 4	+ 15	+ 6
4	+ 4	+ 5	+ 11
5	+ 2	+ 3	+ 4
6	+ 2	+ 4	+ 7
Net income	+ 8	+ 12	+ 11

Which one of these proposals should the directors accept? Project B, because it has the highest net income? The answer is not come by as simply as that. There are, in fact, three general approaches to the problem: measuring return on investment, measuring pay-back period, and applying discount factors. Discounting techniques involve two main methods: net present value, and discounted cash flow (DCF).

Return on Investment

This method, also known as the "rate of return" method, considers the average annual income and compares this with the total investment. In this respect it reflects the "profit to assets" approach with which we began profitability analysis in Chapter 4. The figures used in the project appraisal context differ from the ratio figures in that "profit" means profit accruing to shareholders, and hence excluding the tax payable on it. Assets, of course, means the investment in fixed assets and working capital necessary to get the project started.

The annual return on investment for each of these projects could be as Table 38 shows.

TABLE 38

	Project A	Project B	Project C
Investment	£25,000	£30,000	£25,000
Return (net income)	£8,000	£12,000	£11,000
Life	6 yrs.	6 yrs.	6 yrs.
Average annual return	$\dfrac{8 \times 100}{25 \times 6}$	$\dfrac{12 \times 100}{30 \times 6}$	$\dfrac{11 \times 100}{25 \times 6}$
	$= 5 \cdot 3\%$	$= 6 \cdot 7\%$	$= 7 \cdot 3\%$

These rates of return are averaged over the whole life of the projects, but are, nevertheless, related to the investment at the start of the project. They ignore the fact that the investment is diminishing all the time as cash is flowing back, just as regular mortgage payments reduce the capital debt as well as meeting the interest payments due. The investment in Project A begins at £25,000, and at the end of the 6 years is zero: the investor (Z Ltd.) has been progressively reducing the investment until at the end it has been completely withdrawn. Consequently, the average investment over the project life is (£25,000 + 0) ÷ 2, which is £12,500. The average rate of return on the amount actually invested is therefore exactly double the rates shown in Table 38.

Project A, $10 \cdot 7\%$. Project B, $13 \cdot 3\%$. Project C, $14 \cdot 7\%$.

On these figures alone, project C would be chosen. An overall return on investment figure is a useful measure to use in appraising past operations year by year, but as a guide to the profitability of future operations it is inadequate in two respects: it pays no heed to investment risks and it takes no account of the timing of cash inflows, whether they come early or late in the life of the project. Other methods will go some way towards remedying these deficiencies.

Pay-back

There is inevitably a degree of risk inherent in business investments. Marketing and technical risks must be faced with as much professional insight as the company can muster, and financial risks follow in their wake. The degree of risk may be largely subjective, but there is one aspect of financial risk which can be measured, and that is the period of time which is expected to elapse before the original outlay is recovered. This period is called the pay-back (or "pay-out") period.

The pay-back period for our three projects can be shown (Table 39) by drawing up *cumulative cash inflow* statements.

TABLE 39. Z LTD.

Cumulative Cash Inflows for Projects A, B, and C

	Project A	Project B	Project C
	£'000	£'000	£'000
Original investment	25	30	25
Cumulative Cash Inflows :			
Year 1	11	4	4
2	21	15	8
3	25	30	14
4	29	35	25
5	31	38	29
6	33	42	36

Table 39 shows that project C recovers the initial investment in year 4, whereas projects A and B both achieve pay-back in year 3. This information can usefully be shown on a graph, and Fig. 5 shows how this is done. If market or production conditions are very uncertain, project C would perhaps be disregarded, and either project A or B chosen. Under conditions of great risk, it may be wisest to adopt the project with the shortest pay-back, although this method, too, has disadvantages. It takes no account of what will be earned after the pay-back period; also, even within the

E

pay-back period, it ignores the timing of cash inflows. Some further analysis is needed to make a decision, so the directors of Z Ltd. will now turn to the discounting methods which have attracted a lot of attention in recent years.

Present Value

It was pointed out above that neither the return on investment method nor the pay-back method takes account of the timing of cash inflows, whether they come earlier or later in the project life. The average return on investment, simply because it is an average, will be the same whether the greatest inflow of cash comes during the first half or the second half of the project.

Why is the timing of cash flows important, apart from the need to shorten the period of risk? The answer is that to an investor money is worth more if he can have it today than if he has to wait for it. Money received and invested today yields interest, money received and invested at some future time does not earn interest while the investor waits for it.

An investment of £1 today at 5% compound interest will become £1·05 in one year's time, £1·10 in 2 years, £1·16 in 3 years, and so on. To an investor who can get 5% on his money, it is immaterial whether he receives £1 today, £1·05 one year hence, or £1·10 2 years hence.

We can put this round the other way. One pound 1 year hence is today equivalent to £(1 ÷ 1·05) or £0·952 if the investor could today invest it at 5%. One pound 2 years hence is equivalent to £0·906 today, i.e. £0·906 is the present worth of £1 2 years hence which could if received today, be invested at 5%. One pound 3 years hence will have a present value of £0·863, and so on; the longer we have to wait for the money, the less will its present value be. This notion of money today being worth more than money in the future derives solely from the ability of money to earn interest if invested, and has nothing to do with inflation.

If we apply present values to a series of future cash inflows, we shall be recognizing that early money is preferable to late

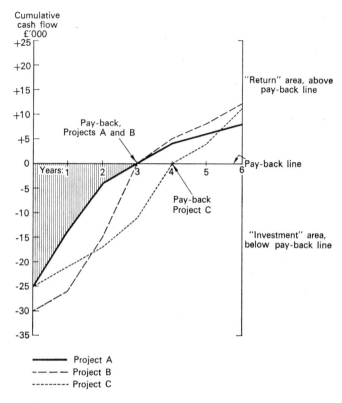

The shaded area shows the amount, duration and
rate of withdrawal of the original investment in Project A

FIG. 5. Cash flow graph; projects A, B, and C.

money. Present values at an assumed rate of interest are simple
to calculate by using discount tables, which give present values of
£1 at varying rates of interest and over different periods of years.
These present values can be used as discount factors to be applied
to amounts other than £1. Before the discount factors can be
applied, it is necessary to decide what is the required earnings rate,

i.e. the rate of compound interest which is either obtainable else-where, or currently being earned by the business, or expected by its financial backers. The required earnings rate is a kind of standard rate of return which the investor thinks he should be able to pull out of a worth-while investment. If the investment proposal does not yield this rate, he will pass it over and look for another opportunity. Just the same reasoning applies to the capital pro-jects under consideration by the directors of Z Ltd.

A generally acceptable earnings rate for industrial projects in the United Kingdom is frequently taken at 10%, and this is the one adopted by Z Ltd. The next document studied by the directors compares the net present value of the three projects, and is shown in Table 40. What does the information on this table signify? It shows what happens when all three projects are measured against a required earnings rate of 10%. What is the significance of these figures?

Project A shows a positive net present value (NPV) of £1368. This is arrived at by adding together the present value of the origi-nal outlay (a negative amount of £25,000, not discounted because the outlay is made now, in year 0 as we called it), and the present values of the cash inflows in succeeding years. The discount fac-tors grow smaller year by year, showing how the present value of £1 diminishes the longer Z Ltd. has to wait for it. The total of all these present values, both negative and positive, is a positive present value of £1368. In effect, the directors of Z Ltd. are saying to the proposer of project A: "On this project you forecast cash inflows of £11,000 in year 1, £10,000 in year 2, and so on. We require 10% return on our capital, and the amount we would have to invest at 10% to yield the cash inflows predicted for your project is £26,368—the sum of the discounted cash inflows for years 1–6 inclusive. However, all you ask us to invest is £25,000. Your pro-posal is an even better investment opportunity than we normally expect to find."

Applying this reasoning to all three projects, the directors might be expected to choose project B, which has the highest net present value of the three, and which can profitably engage a larger sum

TABLE 40. Z LTD.
Net Present Values of Projects A, B, and C
Required earnings rate = 10%

Year	Discount factor for 10%	Project A		Project B		Project C	
		Cash generation	Present value	Cash generation	Present value	Cash generation	Present value
		£	£	£	£	£	£
0	—	− 25,000	− 25,000	− 30,000	− 30,000	− 25,000	− 25,000
1	0·909	+ 11,000	+ 10,000	+ 4,000	+ 3,636	+ 4,000	+ 3,636
2	0·826	+ 10,000	+ 8,260	+ 11,000	+ 9,086	+ 4,000	+ 3,304
3	0·751	+ 4,000	+ 3,004	+ 15,000	+ 11,265	+ 6,000	+ 4,506
4	0·683	+ 4,000	+ 2,732	+ 5,000	+ 3,415	+ 11,000	+ 7,513
5	0·621	+ 2,000	+ 1,242	+ 3,000	+ 1,863	+ 4,000	+ 2,484
6	0·565	+ 2,000	+ 1,130	+ 4,000	+ 2,260	+ 7,000	+ 3,955
Net present value			+ 1,368		+ 1,525		+ 398

than project A, assuming that the required £30,000 is available. However, the project with the higher NPV is the more profitable only when the initial outlays are identical in each project. Where the outlays are different, it is helpful to express NPV as a percentage of initial investment, and compare the resulting ratios (sometimes called a "profitability index") (Table 41).

TABLE 41.

	Project A	Project B
NPV	£1,368	£1,525
Initial outlay	£25,000	£30,000
Ratio	5·47%	5·09%

On this reasoning, project A would be selected. Project C is now ruled out because of the time-lag in cash inflows. Three years of project C would bring in only £14,000, 39% of the total inflows. In project A, the first 3 years are expected to bring in over 75% of total inflows.

Discounted Cash Flow

The present value method described above utilizes discounted cash flows, but the name "discounted cash flow" is one of the names given to an extension of present value technique whereby a rate of return is sought rather than assumed. The DCF method, also called "solution rate of return" or "internal rate of return", is based on the same cash flows as previously used, but instead of merely checking the net present value at the required rate of return, it attempts to find out what the earning power of the investment is, i.e. the rate of return which will bring the NPV nearest to zero. If this solution or internal rate of return is higher than the required earnings rate, and if it is a simple case of acceptance or non-acceptance, then the proposal can be accepted. In competing projects of the same length and involving the same

TABLE 42. PRESENT VALUE OF £1

(All figures are after the decimal point)

Years hence	5%	6%	7%	8%	9%	10%	11%	12%	13%	14%	15%
1	952	943	935	926	917	909	901	893	885	877	870
2	907	890	873	857	842	826	812	797	783	769	756
3	864	840	816	794	772	751	731	712	693	675	658
4	823	792	763	735	708	683	659	636	613	592	572
5	784	747	713	681	650	621	593	567	543	519	497
6	746	705	666	630	596	564	535	507	480	456	432
7	711	665	623	583	547	513	482	452	425	400	376
8	677	627	582	540	502	467	434	404	376	351	327
9	645	592	544	500	460	424	391	361	333	308	284
10	614	558	508	463	422	386	352	322	295	270	247

Note: These tables are compound interest tables in reverse. £1 at 5% will be worth £1·05 1 year hence, and £1 1 year hence will be worth £(1 ÷ 1·05) or £0·952 today, if it can be invested at 5%. The present value of £1 1 year hence at 5% is thus shown above as 0·952. This can be checked: £0·952 × 1·05 = £0·9996 or £1. (The 0·0004 difference is due to rounding the discount factors to only three decimal places.)

TABLE 43. Z LTD.: SEARCH FOR PROJECT A EARNING POWER

Year	Net cash generation	10% Discount factor	10% Present value	11% Discount factor	11% Present value	12% Discount factor	12% Present value	13% Discount factor	13% Present value
	£		£		£		£		£
0	− 25,000	—	− 25,000	—	− 25,000	—	− 25,000	—	− 25,000
1	+ 11,000	·909	+ 10,000	·901	+ 9,911	·893	+ 9,823	·885	+ 9,735
2	+ 10,000	·826	+ 8,260	·812	+ 8,120	·797	+ 7,970	·783	+ 7,830
3	+ 4,000	·751	+ 3,004	·731	+ 2,924	·712	+ 2,848	·693	+ 2,772
4	+ 4,000	·683	+ 2,732	·659	+ 2,636	·636	+ 2,544	·613	+ 2,452
5	+ 2,000	·621	+ 1,242	·594	+ 1,188	·567	+ 1,134	·543	+ 1,086
6	+ 2,000	·565	+ 1,130	·535	+ 1,070	·507	+ 1,014	·480	+ 960
Net present value		—	+ 1,368	—	+ 849	—	+ 333	—	− 165

outlay, the project to be preferred is the one with the highest earning power. Where projects are of different lengths and differing outlays, many analysts feel that comparison of the NPV/ initial outlay ratios will be a better guide.

At this stage, it will be useful to refer to a discount table, and Table 42 shows the present value of £1 at 5% to 15% for periods up to 10 years. Notice how the present values for a given year drop as the rate increases; obviously, the greater the rate of return available, the lower the present value needing to be invested to realize a given amount at the end of a given period. Low rates applied to a cash flow will almost always give a positive NPV. As the rate of return is raised, the discount factors will drop, and the NPV will move towards zero. The rate of return which brings the NPV nearest zero is the solution rate of return, and it measures the earning power of the project because it reveals the highest annual rate of interest which the project can bear while returning the initial input of cash in its entirety.

The solution rate of return or earning power of a project can only be found by a process of trial and error. Table 43 shows the decreasing NPV of project A as the rate of return is raised from 10%.

The earning power of project A is thus taken to be 13%, since this rate of return takes the NPV nearest to zero. By a similar process, the earning power of project B is found to be 12%, and for project C about 10·5%. On these grounds, project A would be preferred.

The solution rate of return can be tested by thinking of project A as a loan made by the directors of Z Ltd., to the project, which agrees to pay back capital and interest at 13% over 6 years in cash instalments as in the predicted cash flow (Table 37). In this way, the project can be treated in financial terms identical with the normal private mortgage (Table 44).

As expected, taking interest at 13% does not leave quite enough to repay the capital.

The search for a solution rate can be helped by graphical methods. If, for example, we were comparing project A and project C, we could plot the NPV of each project at 5%, 10%,

TABLE 44

Year	Capital outstanding at beginning of year	13% interest on capital outstanding	Cash flow	Capital repayment
	£	£	£	£
1	25,000	3,250	11,000	7,750
2	17,250	2,243	10,000	7,757
3	9,493	1,234	4,000	2,766
4	6,727	875	4,000	3,125
5	3,602	458	2,000	1,542
6	2,060	268	2,000	1,732
Total Years 1–6	328[a]	8,328	33,000	24,672

[a] Capital outstanding at end of project if 13% interest is charged.

and 15%. The three points on the graph indicate a curve for each project which will cut the zero NPV line at the solution rate of return. The graph for this comparison is Fig. 6.

Looking back at the four methods, we can see how the directors of Z Ltd., are guided towards a different preference by each method. While discounting techniques seem to offer the most comprehensive basis on which to make long-term decisions, no one method can be said to be the best. In many cases, the effort of applying discount factors may be quite unjustified, if other considerations are sufficient to make it obvious which course should be adopted.

The study of financial techniques should never lead to the view that financial considerations are always the dominant ones. It is as well to know what are the financial implications of business decisions, but it does not follow that the course of action which is most beneficial financially is necessarily the wisest one to adopt. For example, the Directors of Z Ltd., in examining the three projects considered above, would think of the marketing factors, of the pattern of customer relationships which would emerge from each. Project A promises quicker returns than the others,

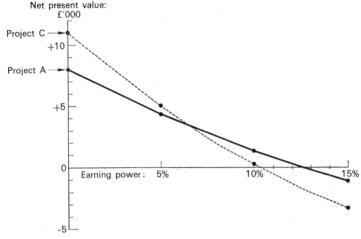

Year	Project A - £				Project C - £			
	Cash flow	D.C.F.,5%	D.C.F.,10%	D.C.F.,15%	Cash flow	D.C.F.,5%	D.C.F.,10%	D.C.F.,15%
0	−25,000	−25,000	−25,000	−25,000	−25,000	−25,000	−25,000	−25,000
1	+11,000	+10,472	+10,000	+9,570	+4,000	+3,808	+3,636	+3,480
2	+10,000	+9,072	+8,260	+7,560	+4,000	+3,628	+3,304	+3,024
3	+4,000	+3,456	+3,004	+2,632	+6,000	+5,184	+4,506	+3,948
4	+4,000	+3,292	+2,732	+2,288	+11,000	+9,053	+7,513	+6,292
5	+2,000	+1,568	+1,242	+994	+4,000	+3,136	+2,484	+1,988
6	+2,000	+1,492	+1,130	+864	+7,000	+5,222	+3,955	+3,024
N.P.V.	8,000	+4,350	+1,368	−1,092	+11,000	+5,031	+398	−3,244

N.B. The net income for each project (Project A, £8,000; Project C £11,000) = The N.P.V. if no interest is charged, i.e., interest at 0%. This gives an extra point on the curve

FIG. 6.

but will the response of the market be too short-lived? Will years 3–6 be a wearisome grind of hard selling or patching up over-used machinery? Project B follows a more normal cycle; steady progress towards peak profits in year 3, winding up in year 6 on a rising curve as plant is disposed of and working capital recovered. But what about project C? It promises steady growth over a long period, with an increasing hold on the market. Perhaps the attention of customers can be retained and turned to other products as project C moves into its final stages.

This kind of thinking needs breadth of vision and business acumen, and the company which combines marketing flair with financial wisdom is in a good position to prosper.

There are some basic considerations to be borne in mind when attempting to appraise the financial viability of alternative business strategies: first, that the cash flow prediction is crucial. A financial analyst in one capital-intensive industry says that he spends 95% of his time making predictions and criticizing other people's predictions; only 5% of time is spent in calculating rates of return. The results of the calculations can obviously be no better than the predictions and assumptions on which they are based. A second point follows from this, that in a soundly run business, making predictions is essential and inescapable. Moreover, these predictions must be made despite the fact that some of the information one would like to have is usually missing. But by carefully noting the assumptions made and comparing them with the conditions which actually emerge, people in business can *improve the accuracy* of the predictions they make. One way of coping with the uncertainty of business conditions is to make three sets of assumptions: best, worst, and most likely.

Summary

Long-term business strategy involves predicting the extent to which money put into capital projects will bring an income to the business, while at the same time keeping the capital sum intact.

Operating income is derived from successful selling, and marketing people are closely involved in the forecast of income likely to be derived from future selling operations.

Traditional methods of appraising the profitability of long-term business projects have tended to concentrate on the average annual rate of return, or on the period of time needed by the project to turn the original outlay back into cash. Newer methods of project appraisal apply discounting techniques (not new in themselves) recognizing that the whole life of the project must be considered, but that early money is worth more than late money.

Financial considerations are not the only ones relevant to business decisions, but they are always important and should be evaluated as accurately as possible.

CHAPTER 6

Looking Ahead:
A Check on Current Operations

THE short-term budgeting described in this chapter assumes that longer-term project planning of the kind described in Chapter 5 has already been carried out; in fact, short- and long-term planning are complementary, and neither is complete without the other.

Of the three long-term projects described in the previous chapter, the directors of Z Ltd., chose project A. During the coming month (July) they will spend £23,000 on new plant and machinery and a further £2000 on stocks, rent, training, and other preliminary expenses related to the project.

As far as current operations are concerned, the directors of Z Ltd., like the idea of quarterly running budgets, so we will describe what happens as they check in detail the financial operations to be carried through in the coming 3 months—July, August, and September.

There are operations of many kinds to think about. Apart from commissioning the new project, there is all the routine purchasing, manufacturing, shop-floor manning, clerical staffing, materials control in the factory, delivery schedules, wages and salaries, factory expenses, office costs, credit control, payments to suppliers, and so on. The problem here is where to start. The budgets to be compiled are obviously interlinked, so which budget should come first?

The answer here lies in the concept of limiting factor. All the above operational activities can be reduced to the three basic business functions: marketing, production, and finance. All three are necessary in a business (though in non-manufacturing firms production may be simply a matter of purchasing) and all three are subject to constraints. No firm can sell unlimited quantities of its products; no firm can manufacture in unlimited quantities, and certainly no firm has unlimited amounts of money at its disposal. The marketing, production, and financial resources available to a company over a given period can each permit a certain level of business activity. Salesmen may be able to sell 1000 units in the period; the factory may be physically equipped to turn out only 800 units, but the working capital available may be able to finance manufacture and delivery of no more than 600 units. At other times, there may be plenty of money available, but only 50 % of factory output can be sold.

To minimize wastage of resources, the management of a firm should recognize its limiting factor and as far as possible balance the other factors with the limiting factor. The first budget to be drawn up, then, should be the budget for the limiting factor. In practice, this is usually sales. If a company is confident of its ability to extend sales, it can usually find financial backers to help it to do so. The capital expenditure programme is itself a part of the process of extending production to the sales limit. Z Ltd. foresaw a possibility of achieving higher sales if it could only manufacture the goods, and since existing capacity was too small, they planned to increase it by investing in project A. In this instance they had the money available from retained profits, but had this not been so they would no doubt have considered external sources.

While finance can usually be found for a good business prospect, it is not available in unlimited quantities. The amount to be used must be in proportion to the income it is hoped to earn. In compiling their budget accounts, therefore, the directors of Z Ltd. must recognize that a given amount of capital employed will be expected to produce an acceptable return, and their financial plans must take account of the three basic ratios described in Chapter 4: profit to assets, sales to assets, and profit to sales. The first budget to construct, therefore, is the budget profit and loss account, which will include the expected revenue from sales, the expenses needed to support the sales programme, and the profit which will accrue as a result. These budget accounts will, of course, be provisional at the first attempt; it may be unrealistic to hope for the turnover and profit originally set down as desirable. Nevertheless, the attempt is worth while if it triggers off the sort of positive thinking which asks "How can we achieve

TABLE 45. Z LTD.

Opening and Budget Balance Sheets, 1 July and 30 September

	1 July (Actual) £	1 July (Actual) £	30 September (Budget) £	30 September (Budget) £
Assets				
Fixed assets at cost	150,000		....	
Less Depreciation to date	40,000		....	
		110,000		....
Current Assets:				
Raw materials	14,000		....	
Work-in-progress	40,000		....	
Finished goods	10,000		....	
Total stock	64,000		....	
Debtors	44,000		....	
Cash and short-term investments	37,000		....	
Total current assets		145,000		....
Total assets		255,000		....
Sources				
Share capital		80,000		....
Reserves		117,000		....
Current liabilities:				
Tax	22,000		....	
Creditors	36,000		....	
Total current liabilities		58,000		....
Total sources		£255,000		....

these turnover and profit goals?" rather than "This is the best we can do; too bad if the return is on the low side."

The financial events envisaged and recorded in these budget accounts will bring about changes in the financial position of the company which will in turn be reflected in a budget balance sheet as at the end of the quarterly period. Use of a proforma balance sheet like the one shown in Table 45 will enable the reader to record these changes and build up for himself a comprehensive picture of the budgeted flow of funds as decisions are made and detailed targets agreed in each operating area.

After a good deal of discussion with the sales manager, the production manager, and the chief accountant, the board of Z Ltd. finally accepted a budget profit and loss account for the July–September quarter (Table 46).

TABLE 46. Z LTD.

Budget Profit and Loss Account, July–September

	£	£
Sales		150,000
Cost of goods sold		108,000
Gross profit		42,000
Selling and distribution expenses	7,500	
General administration expenses	12,500	
		20,000
Net profit before tax		22,000
Tax (40%)		8,800
Net profit after tax		£13,200

This budget profit and loss statement takes account of the new project which will be launched during the quarter. Subsidiary records will be kept to watch the progress of this project, i.e. to compare the actual cash generation with the cash flow forecasts which were examined in detail earlier in the year.

The process of budgeting is at the heart of financial control, and our next task is to examine the budget profit and loss figures one by one. Two aspects of the budget process should emerge: first, the problem of comparing the costs of future activity with the likely benefits to be derived from it (a problem particularly acute in the marketing area), and, secondly, the unifying influence of the money measure.

Sales, £150,000

The sales forecast is obviously the main determinant of business activity, and is the result of a detailed study of customer needs, preferences, awareness of available products, and response to the marketing effort put out by Z Ltd. This marketing effort will result from the company's marketing philosophy, combined with policy decisions on production capacity, costs and selling prices. The techniques of marketing as such are described in other books in this series, and must here be taken for granted. The relationship between sales volume, costs, and prices is of particular interest to marketing people and will be examined in the next chapter. For our present purpose, it is sufficient to note that sales of given products in given quantities and at given prices are thought to be possible and desirable, and that the revenue resulting from such sales will amount to £150,000.

Cost of goods sold, £108,000

This figure is the predicted ex-works cost of goods which will be dispatched during the quarter. The ex-works cost is largely the responsibility of the production manager, who controls the flow of materials through the works and the manufacturing effort applied to the raw materials as they are transformed into finished goods.

The check points in the production process are the three stock accounts—raw materials, work-in-progress, and finished goods. We saw how an historical cost of goods sold figure was built up in Chapter 3, and the production budgeting process works in much the same way but in a reverse direction. A production budget is essentially three budgeted stock accounts, and these are shown in Table 47 in relation to the current plans of Z Ltd. The narrative attached to the figures has been expanded to show how the production manager explains and discusses the budgets with the people who work with him at the factory.

Note that before the production manager of Z Ltd. can compile his budget he needs answers to two questions: (a) What goods will our customers hope to receive during the quarter?, and (b) What stock levels are necessary to achieve these and future deliveries? In other words, he builds his production budget on the sales budget and the stock budgets. Stocks are the buffer between production and sales, and marketing predictions obviously play a large part in determining appropriate stock levels.

The production budget figures read with a deceptive ease. Behind every one of them are detailed schedules compiled by section foremen, production planning staff, personnel officers, and so on, each deciding what his particular section will contribute to the production effort and how much it should cost. And behind these schedules lie meetings, discussions, research, calculations,

TABLE 47. Z LTD.
Stock and Production Budgets, July–September

Stock budget: To support current and future sales programmes, and to optimize buying prices, utilization of factory floor space etc., it is expected that the value of stocks held at the end of the current quarter will be as follows:

	Value	Increase during period	
		£	% on opening stock
	£		
Raw material	18,000	4,000	29
Work-in-progress	50,000	10,000	25
Finished goods	12,000	2,000	20
Total	80,000	16,000	25

Table 47. Z Ltd.—*cont.*

Production budget: Warehouse Manager

		£
Customers will require delivery of goods, production cost of which is		108,000
We must also have finished goods in the warehouse at 30 Sept. costing		12,000
So we must provide finished goods to the cost value of		120,000
But we begin the quarter with finished goods in stock at		10,000
So the cost of finished goods to pass from shop-floor to warehouse need be only		£110,000

Production budget: Production Superintendent

	£
We must complete the manufacture of products costing	110,000
We must also have jobs in hand in the production shops at 30 September costing	50,000
So we must handle work-in-progress to the cost value of	160,000
But we begin the quarter with jobs already in hand to the cost value of	40,000
So the cost of the work we shall actually do this quarter will be only	120,000
Of which direct wages (£42,000) and factory overheads (£19,000) will account for	61,000
Leaving the remainder as the value of raw materials to be drawn from stores	£59,000

Production budget: Materials Controller

	£
Issues of raw materials to the shop floor will be costed at	59,000
We must also have raw materials in the stores at 30 September costing	18,000
So we must provide a total supply of raw materials costing	77,000
But we begin the quarter with stock at a cost value of	14,000
So all we need to purchase is raw materials costing	£63,000

negotiations on quantity and quality standards, and so on. The final figures reflect a measure of agreement on what each part of the factory organization will attempt to achieve during the July–September quarter.

Selling and distribution expenses, £7500

How much should a marketing department spend in doing its job, i.e. getting orders, delivering the goods, and maintaining customer satisfaction?* This is a particularly thorny problem, since a company faced with declining sales, and therefore declining cash inflows, may nevertheless need to spend more on order-getting. At the best of times, the benefits of particular order-getting activities are difficult to correlate with the costs. All of this stems from the simple fact first mentioned in Chapter 1, that the decision whether or not to place an order lies outside the selling company, and traditional methods of control, based largely on the use of authority, cannot be used to influence that decision. This is undoubtedly a reason why some companies, rather than develop their skill in non-authoritarian control, choose instead to buy up their outlets.

How did Z Ltd. arrive at their decision to accept £7500 as an appropriate budget for selling and distribution expenses during July, August, and September? Distribution costs were, of course, the easier part; the Warehouse Manager, perhaps, applied some transport costings to the £108,000 worth of goods which were to be dispatched, and after considering mode of transport, distance, and cost per ton/mile, came up with an acceptable forecast. But the order-getting costs are different. They are "discretionary" costs to some extent: management can decide, period by period, how much or how little to spend, hoping that the orders will flow in as needed.

It is not possible to give rules of thumb on the question of order-getting costs; companies must simply analyse "all those

* The Institute of Marketing has recently produced a new definition of marketing which says the same thing with greater precision. Marketing is defined as "The management function which organizes and directs all those business activities involved in assessing and converting customer purchasing power into effective demand for a specific product or service, and in moving the product or service to the final consumer or user so as to achieve the profit target or other objective set by the company" (*Financial Times*, 11 October 1966). This definition bears out what was said earlier about financial considerations not being the only ones.

business activities involved in converting customer purchasing power into demand for a specific product", watch carefully the results which can truly be ascribed to particular activities, and endeavour to repeat success. Economic analysis and probability statistics will help, but these subjects need books on their own.

It might be helpful, however, to describe three possible approaches to the problem which have been tried by different firms. In one firm, it was accepted that there could be no direct relationship between order-getting costs and volume of orders obtained. The marketing effort of the company was only one influence among many which caused the customer to place an order. Whether or not he did so depended to a great extent on his ability or wish to buy, and these things were determined largely by his forward buying policy, liquidity, and by his own order book if he himself were also in business. The economic climate, the efforts of competitors, and the general reputation of the company also influenced a potential customer. Reputation followed mainly from the degree of satisfaction which customers had derived in the past from the company's products, or heard about from the experience of other users. This degree of satisfaction was related to many things outside the direct control of the selling department, i.e. design, quality control, and adherence to promised delivery dates. As a result of these factors, it was thought impossible in this firm to provide quantitative measurements of the efficiency of the sales department, or to hold it to a "correct" level of selling expense.

While recognizing that there were no objective criteria for judging actual selling costs, the company nevertheless used such devices as keyed advertisements, average cost per salesman's call, average daily calls, average daily travelling costs, etc., to provide some assistance to marketing executives in their attempts to justify the main items of expenditure. But clearly no salesman would be expected to refrain from calling on a reasonable prospect merely because to do so would put his travelling costs over the daily average.

The management of the second firm took a different view. The chief executive of this firm, whose working life in the company had been mainly in production, was dissatisfied with the lack of objective criteria for judging the reasonableness of the selling expense estimates. He thought that selling expenses could best be controlled by treating them like production costs and considering them as either fixed or variable. He asked for some research to be done into the cost records of previous years to see how the different items of selling cost had varied in relation to the volume of business. As a result of this research, the degree of variability, if any, was established for each item of selling expense. The fixed part of each item was also established by determining the capacity level below which the company would be unlikely to operate, and assuming that expenses at this level would be independent of fluctuations in volume. Monthly budget statements were proposed in which actual selling expenses were compared with a variable budget, adjusted to the actual volume of sales achieved. The old monthly budgets had been based on a one-twelfth apportionment of the budgeted selling expenses for a complete year. With the proposed variable budgets, a poor sales result threw up an overspending above budget, while good months tended to show spending below budget.

The sales force in this firm was not impressed with the proposals. Like their opposite numbers in the previous firm, they realized that customers bought or refrained from buying for reasons largely unconnected with the efforts made and costs incurred by the sales organization.

The third company took a different view again. The management of this company recognized that people have great potentialities for growth, and will in the right conditions perform much better if they are given genuine and significant responsibility for their own achievements. This firm threw out its assembly lines and organized production on the basis of small teams each running their own part of the business. Selling expenses were controlled in accordance with the same philosophy. Every salesman was given a flat expense allowance big enough to cover all reasonable travelling, car, lodging, and entertainment expenses. The allowance permitted him to replace his car every 2 years if he wished. If he could do his job and spend less than the allowance, he was free to pocket the difference. No expense forms had to be submitted.

During the 3 years following the introduction of these arrangements, production and sales doubled, and the company captured 50% of a highly competitive market.* Obviously, this did not stem simply from the generous flat-rate allowance to salesmen. Perhaps this form of selling expense control is only for the company which can afford it, but at any rate it is far simpler to operate than the fixed-variable procedure described previously.

The great unknown in selling expenditure is, of course, advertising, unknown in the sense that its effects and benefits are difficult to isolate. There is a vague feeling in certain quarters (e.g. consumer associations) that advertising expenditure is wasteful and unnecessary, and that many products would be bought in the same quantities if they were not advertised or were advertised far less. Particularly would this be so if the producers reduced their prices by an amount corresponding with the saving in advertising costs.

However, marketing people still talk about the firmly established household product which ceased to advertise. It continued to sell satisfactorily for about 2 years, and then suddenly and irretrievably ceased to be purchased. It was eventually swamped by other, well-advertised, products. Advertising costs will continue to figure in business budgets, the amount involved bearing some relationship to the intensity of competition or the difficulty of operating up to capacity level or both. Clearly, however, whatever the form of budgetary control, nothing is gained by attempting to compare monthly advertising costs with monthly volume of business.

It goes without saying that a company must be able to afford its advertising appropriation. This may involve the harsh problem

* Reported in *Reader's Digest*, December 1963, in an article by Vance Packard entitled "A chance for everyone to grow".

of finding money to buy your way out of a sales drop, when, by definition, cash is dwindling. A businessman in this position can either (a) use existing cash resources, possibly straining credit to dangerous limits, or (b) introduce extra cash into the business, if he has it available, and still believes in his product, or (c) do nothing and hope for the best, or (d) go out of business, either on his own initiative or that of his creditors. The situation is obviously far better avoided altogether. The biggest help in avoiding it is careful cash budgeting, which we shall come to later in this chapter.

General administration expenses, £12,500

These are the central office costs—telephone, rent, light, heat, stationery, and so on, together with what is usually the largest single item of administration cost—salaries and related expenditure. There are ways and means of controlling office costs which are growing in refinement and usefulness. Worth-while methods are based on an analysis of the office work which *needs* to be done. The essential office procedure in any firm is the one which links order and invoice; other procedures may precede this one (e.g. inquiries and quotations) or round it off (sales ledger and statements), and together these make up the "main-line" information system. The aim of this system is to provide the information needed to supply what it is the customer wants and to secure the return flow of cash. It is a "loop" system of documentation which originates with the customer, passes through the firm, and returns to him in the form of an invoice. Linked with this main-line system are the internal control systems, consisting of essential flow documents and records. These systems should stem from deliberate control policies which insist on the usefulness of the information to be provided. (Frequently one finds elaborate and unnecessary control systems which were installed in a mood of insecurity following mistakes or errors of judgement.) Lubricating this basic documentary flow is the *ad hoc* paperwork of letters and memos, the written communications which are a necessary supplement to oral interpersonal communication. In the final chapter we shall discuss more fully the information needs of marketing personnel in so far as they are relevant to financial control. For the moment it is sufficient to note that the general administration overhead figure is what it is mainly because of the information processing needs of the business. If ratios show that this figure is absorbing an increasing amount of sales revenue, management needs to ask, "What benefits are we getting from these costs?" Optimization of office costs and improving office services should be a routine task in every business, and specialist services are available to help.

Sometimes financial charges, such as loan interest, are included in general administration costs, sometimes shown separately. In the type of business we are considering (one making and selling its own products) financial transactions arising from loans and investments are outside the main area of operations and it is preferable to budget and report them separately.

Net profit before tax, £22,000

This is the residual operating profit which will be achieved if the sales budget is met and costs are held to budget levels. Broadly speaking, the operating management of the business has done its job if it achieves a satisfactory net profit before tax figure—which would not necessarily be that shown in the budget.

Tax, £8800, *and net profit after tax*, £13,200

Company profits currently bear a corporation tax of 40%. In addition, income tax at 8s. 3d. in the £ is payable by the company (and therefore by its shareholders), on all distributed profits. The taxable profit is arrived at in accordance with government regulations whereby certain expenses which a company might include in its final accounts are not accepted as business expenses by the Inland Revenue. Examples of these are charitable subscriptions, political donations, and entertaining expenses, unless in respect of potential overseas buyers. In practice, the ordinary profit and taxable profit figures may not be significantly different, and for operating budget purposes, it is sufficient to deduct a straight 40% from net profit before tax without attempting to prejudge the allowability of expenses or the distribution of profit.

With the budget profit and loss account satisfactorily worked out, the budget balance sheet as at 30 September can begin to take shape. Before we turn to the balance sheet, however, it will be useful to mention the capital expenditure budget, which will also affect the balance sheet.

The capital budget must take account of disposals as well as acquisition of fixed assets. Disposals involve removing from the company's records the original cost of the assets disposed of, the accumulated depreciation on the assets, and their book value at the time of disposal. The capital account (usually capital reserve account if there is one) must also be adjusted to take account of any profits or losses on disposal. If a machine costing £100 has been depreciated by £80 down to £20 and is then sold for £30, the owners of the business have made a capital profit of £10. The actual cost of the machine to the firm has been £100 less £30, i.e. £70, but the revenue profits of the business have been charged £80. The difference of £10 has to be added back to the ownership capital, or the sources will be understated, and the balance sheet will not balance. On the assets side, £30 of additional cash will enter current assets when the machine is sold, but only £20 will be deducted from the book value of fixed assets. Total assets will therefore rise by £10, and this must be balanced by a corresponding rise of £10 in ownership capital.

Inside Z Ltd., the directors are getting rid of a piece of machinery no longer wanted. A few years back it was bought for £5000, and its book value is now £2000. However, another firm has agreed to buy it for £3000. It has also been agreed that the depreciation charge on the fixed assets which continue to be used (including the new project A plant) will be £4000 for the July–September quarter. The fixed asset budget will look like Table 48.

TABLE 48. Z LTD.

Fixed Asset Budget, July–September

	Acquisition cost	Depreciation to date	Book value
	£	£	£
As in opening balance sheet	150,000	40,000	110,000
Acquisitions during period	23,000	—	23,000
	173,000	40,000	133,000
Less Disposals	5,000	3,000	2,000
	168,000	37,000	131,000
Depreciation during period	—	+ 4,000	− 4,000
As in closing (budget) balance sheet	£168,000	£41,000	£127,000

With some clear financial targets to aim at, and with its sales, production, purchasing, stock, and fixed asset budgets neatly tied up, Z Ltd. looks all set to get started on operations for the coming quarter. But not all the loose ends are tied up yet. The budget balance sheet is not yet complete, as we shall see when we put in the budget figures so far calculated. Table 49 shows the budget balance sheet with the fixed asset adjustments (Table 48), budget stock levels (Table 47), share capital (unchanged), reserves (see below) and taxation (Table 46).

The reserves of £117,000 are increased first by the £13,200 net profit after tax and also by the £1000 profit on disposal of the machinery. This explains the budget figure of £131,200.

There are now only three figures missing from the budget balance sheet: cash (including short-term investments), debtors, and creditors. The need to forecast how these figures will change brings us to the important topic of cash budgeting, important because in the cash budget lie the company's plans for remaining liquid. The importance of liquidity has already been stressed: insufficient liquidity can bring a business to a halt no matter how impressive its long-term plans. But there is no need for people in business to become obsessed with this simple fact of life; accurate cash forecasting should be sufficient to allay fears and suggest any necessary action well before the situation gets out of hand. When Rolls Razor went out of business in 1964 it was stated by one of the investigating accountants that the company had been undercapitalized, and needed additional long-term cash. "It may have been", went the report "that if the

TABLE 49. Z LTD.

Opening and Budget Balance Sheets, 1 July and 30 September

	1 July (actual)		30 September (Budget)	
	£	£	£	£
Assets				
Fixed assets at cost	150,000		168,000	
Less Depreciation to date	40,000		41,000	
		110,000		127,000
Current assets:				
Raw materials	14,000		18,000	
Work-in-progress	40,000		50,000	
Finished goods	10,000		12,000	
Total stock	64,000		80,000	
Debtors	44,000		....	
Cash and short-term investments	37,000		....	
Total current assets		145,000		....
Total assets		£255,000		£........
Sources				
Share capital		80,000		80,000
Reserves		117,000		131,200
Current liabilities:				
Tax	22,000		8,800	
Creditors	36,000		....	
Total current liabilities		58,000		....
Total sources		£255,000		£

directors had proper cash forecasts and raised money when they were trading successfully, the present situation might never have arisen."

To forecast the flow of cash through Z Ltd., in the coming 3 months we must construct a debtors' budget, a creditors' budget, and finally a cash budget in which all foreseeable receipts and payments will be brought together.

The debtors' budget answers the questions, "What credit sales shall we make during the period, and when can we expect to receive the money for these credit sales?" The first question has already been answered in the budget profit and loss account (Table 46), Z Ltd. having no cash sales. To the credit sales figure of £150,000 must, of course, be added the existing debtors on the company's books at 1st July. The second question can only be answered by examining the response of customers to the firm's debt-collection policy. (Note that the response is what counts rather than the policy.) To discover this we have to analyse the sales ledger accounts from time to time to check the payment pattern. Let us assume that 90% of amounts owing to Z Ltd. are paid during the month following delivery and 10% during the second month after delivery. This knowledge applied to the forecasts of monthly deliveries will enable the chief accountant to construct the debtors' budget, which is shown in Table 50 (a).

The creditors' budget is drawn up in a similar way, and is shown in Table 50 (b). This time we find that the payment policy of Z Ltd. is a little slower than its collection policy, and is normally 70% during first month after receipt of goods or service, 20% during second month, and 10% during third month. The figure of purchases for the period, £63,000, is the figure arrived at in the production budget of Table 48.

The creditors will in fact decrease during the period, despite the expanding sales. This may be a result of a higher than normal usage of materials earlier in the year, and if this were so, it would explain the fairly heavy payments to be made during July in respect of April and May purchases.

TABLE 50. Z LTD.

(a) *Debtors' Budget, July–September*

	July	August	September	Period
	£	£	£	£
Debtors at start of period	44,000	44,000	54,000	44,000
Add Credit sales	40,000	50,000	60,000	150,000
Sub-total	84,000	94,000	114,000	194,000
Less Cash received in respect of:				
May deliveries	4,000	—	—	4,000
June deliveries	36,000	4,000	—	40,000
July deliveries	—	36,000	4,000	40,000
August deliveries	—	—	45,000	45,000
Total cash received	40,000	40,000	49,000	129,000
Debtors at end of period	44,000	54,000	65,000	65,000

(b) *Creditors' Budget, July–September*

	July	August	September	Period
	£	£	£	£
Creditors at start of period	36,000	28,000	27,400	36,000
Add Purchases	18,000	20,000	25,000	63,000
Sub-total	54,000	48,000	52,400	99,000
Less Cash paid in respect of:				
April purchases	4,000	—	—	4,000
May purchases	8,000	4,000	—	12,000
June purchases	14,000	4,000	2,000	20,000
July purchases	—	12,600	3,600	16,200
August purchases	—	—	14,000	14,000
Total cash paid	26,000	20,600	19,600	66,200
Creditors at end of period	28,000	27,400	32,800	32,800

TABLE 51. Z LTD.

Cash Budget, July–September

Item	£	Source
Opening balance	37,000	Opening balance sheet (Table 45)
Add Receipts:		
Sales	129,000	Debtors' budget (Table 50 (a))
Disposal of machinery	3,000	Fixed asset budget (Table 48)
Total cash available	169,000	
Deduct Payments:		
Purchases	66,200	Creditors' budget (Table 50 (b))
Wages	42,000	Production budget (Table 47)
Factory overheads	15,000	Production budget and fixed asset budget
Selling and distribution	7,500	Profit and loss account budget (Table 46)
General administration	12,500	Profit and loss account budget
Fixed assets	23,000	Fixed asset budget
Total payments	166,200	
Closing balance	2,800	

We now have all the information needed to draw up the cash budget itself (Table 51).

One figure in the cash budget needs a word of explanation. The factory overhead figure of £15,000 does not correspond with the figure anticipated in the production budget, which showed an amount of £19,000. The reason for the difference is the depreciation charge of £4,000, rightly included as a factory overhead, but not, of course, needing to be paid out in cash.

At this point the directors might well heave a sigh of relief: cash is adequate to meet the strain of expansion, and the cash balance at 30 September, though meagre, should rise during the following quarter as customers pay their debts. However, one further check would be wise. We can get from the responsible executives an estimate of how these cash receipts and payments will be phased over the 3 months of the period. A phased cash budget will give the directors a final and useful check on the liquidity of Z Ltd., and could be drawn up in the form of Table 52.

TABLE 52. Z LTD.

Phased Cash Budget, July–September

Item	July	August	September	Period
Opening balance	37,000	28,000	− 1,600	37,000
Add Receipts:				
Sales	40,000	40,000	49,000	129,000
Disposal of machinery	—	—	3,000	3,000
Total cash available	77,000	68,000	50,400	169,000
Deduct Payments:				
Purchases	26,000	20,600	19,600	66,200
Wages	13,000	14,000	15,000	42,000
Factory overheads	4,000	4,500	6,500	15,000
Selling and distribution	2,000	3,500	2,000	7,500
General administration	4,000	4,000	4,500	12,500
Fixed assets	—	23,000	—	23,000
Total payments	49,000	69,600	47,600	166,200
Closing balance	28,000	− 1,600	2,800	+ 2,800

The phased cash budget shows that at the end of August there will be a small deficiency of cash. The directors have a number of alternatives open to them. Can they delay payment of creditors? The average payment period is already budgeted at 48 days,* so this might not be a good move. Can they delay selling costs planned for August? Or persuade the firm buying the unwanted machine to pay a little earlier? Or ask for an overdraft? Whatever course they adopt is not of immediate concern to us; it is sufficient to note that the phased cash budget alerts the directors to the

* Calculated, as explained on p. 89, i.e. creditors at end of period (£32,800) ÷ purchases during period (£63,000) × no. of days in period (92).

possibility of a temporary cash shortage in sufficient time for them to take whatever corrective action they think necessary.

The budget balance sheet can now be completed by inserting the final balances of cash, debtors and creditors. Table 53 gives this information, and with the budget forecast of what the financial position of the company will probably be like in 3 months' time, the formal process of compiling budget accounts is at an end.

TABLE 53. Z LTD.

Opening and Budget Balance Sheets, 1 July and 30 September

	1 July (actual)		30 September (budget)	
	£	£	£	£
Assets				
Fixed assets at cost	150,000		168,000	
Less Depreciation to date	40,000		41,000	
		110,000		127,000
Current assets:				
Raw materials	14,000		18,000	
Work-in-progress	40,000		50,000	
Finished goods	10,000		12,000	
Total stock	64,000		80,000	
Debtors	44,000		65,000	
Cash and short-term investments	37,000		2,800	
Total current assets		145,000		147,800
Total assets		£255,000		£274,800
Sources				
Share capital		80,000		80,000
Reserves		117,000		131,200
Current liabilities:				
Tax	22,000		30,800	
Creditors	36,000		32,800	
Total current liabilities		58,000		63,600
Total sources		£255,000		£274,800

The financial viability of the company's plans can be tested by exploring the relationships between some of the budget account items. The ratios will relate to operations over a period of only 3 months, which will give much lower turnover and profit generation ratios than ratios covering a whole year. The budget balance sheet and profit and loss account indicate that Z Ltd. hopes for a profit to assets ratio of 8%, with an asset turnover of 0·55 times during the quarter and a profit to sales ratio of 14·7%. The planned distribution of the sales is as follows: production costs, 72%; selling and distribution costs, 5%; general administration costs, 8·5%; profit before tax, 14·5%. Finished goods in stock at 30 September will equal about 1½ weeks' deliveries. Total stocks will be sufficient to sustain about 9½ weeks' operations, provided the mix of items actually in the stores is the one required by the production schedules. These figures by themselves mean little. They must always be compared with what the management

TABLE 54. Z Ltd.

Budgeted Funds flow Statement, July–September

	£	£
Sources:		
Funds from operations		17,200
Proceeds from sale of fixed assets		3,000
Decrease in working capital		2,800 ←
		23,000
Application: New fixed assets		23,000
Analysis of working capital changes		
Sources:		
Decrease in cash, etc.	34,200	
Increase in tax	8,800	
		43,000
Less Applications:		
Increase in stocks	16,000	
Increase in debtors	21,000	
Decrease in creditors	3,200	
		40,200
Net decrease in working capital		£2,800 ←

of the firm believes to be possible and desirable developments in the firm's achievements.

Another useful check on budget plans is the budget funds-flow statement. Comparison of the opening and budget balance sheets, together with additional information already given, will enable a budget funds statement to be drawn up as shown in Table 54.

This budget funds-flow statement is in slightly different form from the one illustrated in Chapter 4, but follows exactly the same principles. Funds to be derived from operations will be the net profit after tax (£13,200) plus depreciation (£4000), i.e. £17,200. Disposal of fixed assets will bring in £3000, and £2800 will be taken from working capital. These three sources provide the £23,000 which will be applied to the new fixed assets required for project A.

For funds-flow purposes, tax has been treated as a current liability. The working capital change, a decrease of £2800, corresponds with the balance-sheet difference between working capital at 1 July and as budgeted for 30 September (Table 55).

TABLE 55

	Current assets	Current liabilities	Working capital
	£	£	£
1 July	145,000	58,000	87,000
30 September	147,800	63,600	84,200
Difference	+ 2,800	+ 5,600	− 2,800

The funds-flow budget puts the financial strategy of expansion in a new light. On the face of it, the cash and readily cashable securities of £38,000 in hand on 1 July seem more than adequate to embark on a capital scheme requiring only £25,000. But, in fact, sales and production plans will involve financing stocks and debtors to the tune of £37,000, plus a further £3200 to keep up to date on payments to suppliers. The increase in tax due can, of course, offer temporary finance.

After looking at their cash budget and proposed funds flow, the directors of Z Ltd. are probably very glad that they did not choose project B, which would have cost £30,000 to launch.

So much for the essential budget accounts needed to check on current business operations. The comments which follow are intended as a guide on how they should be used.

First it is impossible to overstress the need for business men to take a predictive view of events, particularly financial events. We can leave the accountants to sort out the past, and when they report their findings they will be better understood if the contents of Chapters 2–4 have been carefully assimilated. But for the manager, and particularly the marketing manager, controllable events lie in the future, and the financial skill required is largely that of comparing the different financial effects of alternative courses of action.

Undoubtedly, marketing and financial considerations loom very large in business planning. The first BBC further education series on "The Managers" devoted programme four to business objectives, and the interviews and discussions were mainly in the financial and marketing area. One managing director spoke at some length on the three basic ratios, profit to assets, profit to sales, and sales to assets. In no sense did the programme claim to be a representative sample of management approaches, but the concern for financial planning, budgeting, and market possibilities was not untypical.

But a note of caution is necessary. There is, to many people, an inherent fascination in the manipulation of a set of interlocking figures which generate other figures, disentangle themselves into various categories, and eventually distil a balance sheet which still balances. Satisfying though this process may be to the figure-minded, it has no value in itself, nor will detailed and elaborate calculations, in themselves, make an extra pennyworth of sales. The object of budget accounts is to clarify targets and demonstrate the interdependence of the different sections of the business. Clarification of targets is in itself a powerful form of motivation, and if budget accounts do not help to motivate people in the required direction, it would be better not to waste time on them.

We must be clear, however, that budget targets can only be provisional targets. They are provisional because they are necessarily based on assumptions about what conditions will be like when the budget period is actually reached. A rigid adherence to budget figures as the only possible criterion of success will tend to show up as failures those who have wrestled expertly with unforeseen difficulties, or allow poor performance to slip by unnoticed. Achieving the budget should never be an end in itself, despite the understandable reluctance of accountants and managers to tear up calculations on which they may have worked long and hard. If a better business opportunity presents itself than was envisaged at budgeting time, then the budget should be either adjusted or abandoned.

The problem of management information systems in a rapidly changing business world is a complex one of great topical interest, and we shall return to it in the final chapter.

One of the biggest uncertainties in forward planning will always be the volume of business activity, i.e. the volume of sales which will be achieved. Indeed, one of the greatest certainties in business is that there will be fluctuations in sales volume. The effect of volume fluctuations on costs, selling prices, and profits, and the need for flexibility in budgeting for sales turnover, will be explained in the next chapter.

Summary

An interlocking system of budget accounts is the best way of checking comprehensively the financial viability of business operations proposed for the immediate future. The process of budgeting involves adding financial values to the results which managers hope to get.

The essential budget accounts needed to check current operations in a manufacturing and marketing business are:

Budget balance sheet.
Budget profit and loss Account:
    Sales forecast.
    Stock budgets.
    Production budget.
    Selling and distribution expense budget.
    General administrative expense budget.

Fixed asset budget.
Debtors' budget.
Creditors' budget.
Cash budget.
Budget ratios and funds flow.

The starting point of financial planning is the balance sheet as at the beginning of the budget period. This opening balance sheet lists the resources owned by the business and with which the management is equipped as it faces the opportunities of the coming budget period.

Planned operations are summarized in the budget profit and loss account in which the volume of sales is compared with a provisional estimate of the likely costs of achieving those sales. These estimates are based on decisions concerning the stock levels and the production, purchasing, selling, and administrative activities appropriate to the sales programme.

It is also essential to check that sufficient cash is available to carry through the programme. The flow of cash through the business depends on expenditure decisions made by management, credit allowed by suppliers of goods and services, and the response of customers to the firm's debt collection policy.

Financial achievements in the different operating areas are summarized and linked together in the budget balance sheet as at the end of the budget period.

Despite the intricate structure of budget accounts, budgets must be sufficiently flexible to permit progressive adjustment of financial targets.

CHAPTER 7

Costs, Selling Price, and Uncertain Demand

IN THIS chapter we shall follow the fortunes of X Ltd., a company which makes and sells a well-known brand of fountain pen. The current budgets have just been compiled, and a group of managers is looking at a summary profit and loss account (Table 56).

TABLE 56. X LTD.

Budget Profit and Loss Account, 1st Quarter

	£
Sales	100,000
Total costs	85,000
Profit	£15,000

This looks promising. Then one of the managers asks, "Suppose we don't achieve sales of £100,000. Suppose sales are only £80,000. What happens to our profit? What profit do we make on sales of, say, £120,000?"

Since profit is the net income accruing after all costs have been met, the answer to this question must be sought in the behaviour of costs during periods of fluctuating business activity. And the salient fact about costs is this: when the volume of business activity fluctuates, some costs tend to vary in sympathy with the fluctuations in volume, while other costs tend to remain unchanged. For example, the cost of the material used in making the product (called "direct material") will clearly increase as the number of units made and sold increases. So will the direct labour cost, and many of the costs of running the production machinery. On the other hand, the factory rent and rates and the works manager's salary will not be directly affected by fluctuations in volume of business. Costs which tend to vary with changes in volume are known as variable costs, and costs unaffected by volume changes are called fixed costs.

The problem of segregating costs into fixed and variable were touched on in the previous chapter in relation to selling costs. Whatever the difficulties of deciding which costs are variable, and by how much, it is certain that most businesses do, in fact, incur costs of each type, and will make a better job of budgeting and cost control the more they know about cost behaviour. One problem is, of course, the grey area of semi-variable costs, costs which are partly variable but contain a fixed element. Every car owner knows that the cost of running a car is a semi-variable cost; taken over a year, part of the cost is fixed (road tax, insurance, perhaps garaging) and part is variable (petrol, oil, maintenance). The fixed costs are incurred regardless of how many miles are driven, while the variable costs are directly proportional to the mileage.

Accounting research into past costs, plus a careful look at future conditions, can usually give a reliable guide as to the incidence of fixed and variable costs inside a given business. Two extremes are theoretically possible: all costs are variable, or all costs are fixed. But most firms incur a mixture of both, and it is the purpose of this chapter to show how useful it is to understand the way in which variable costs, fixed costs, selling prices, and volume of business interact to determine the level of profit achieved.

Cost–price–volume relationships are at the heart of such financial techniques as direct costing, marginal costing and break-even analysis. Though related, these techniques are distinct. Despite the lack of a universally accepted terminology, there is a wide and reliable consensus of opinion which understands these different techniques as follows:

(a) *Direct costing*: a system of recording and reporting costs in which fixed and variable costs are segregated and only variable production expenses (or "direct expenses") are added to raw material costs to arrive at work-in-progress and finished goods stock values; fixed costs are written off in the profit and loss account of the period in which they are incurred, and not carried forward to the period in which the goods are sold.

(b) *Marginal costing*: an approach to financial decision-making (rather than a continuous accounting system) whereby the attention of management is drawn to the effect which changes in volume and type of output have on costs and revenues. Such an approach will often be used in the solution of specific problems.

(c) *Break-even analysis*: the technique which, by distinguishing between fixed and variable costs, seeks to establish a theoretical level of sales at which neither profit nor loss will be made. It answers the question "How far can sales drop before we start making a loss?"

The marginal approach to cost control and profit planning focuses attention on the analysis of sales revenue as follows: (a) from the selling price of one unit of the product deduct the variable costs of producing and distributing one unit; these will be the costs which vary in direct proportion to sales; (b) this leaves a difference or "margin" which is a contribution to fixed

TABLE 57. X LTD.

Budget Profit and Loss Account, 1st Quarter

	£
Sales (100,000 units at 20*s*. each)	100,000
Variable costs (12*s*. per unit)	60,000
Total contribution (8*s*. per unit)	40,000
Fixed costs	25,000
Net profit	£15,000

overheads; (c) add together all unit contributions to provide a fund from which fixed costs will be met; (d) from the total contribution deduct total fixed costs to show net profit, or, if fixed costs exceed total contribution, net loss.

The budget plans of X Ltd. can be analysed in marginal terms as Table 57 shows.

Uncertainty of demand requires a study of the effect of volume changes on profits given the present cost and price structure. A good way of doing this is to draw a break-even chart, which is a graph showing sales value and costs at different levels of volume. This is how you could draw a break-even chart for X Ltd.:

1. Plot sales value and cost on the *y* (vertical) axis and levels of volume on the *x* (horizontal) axis. A convenient measure of volume is the sales value itself, though other measures, such as quantity of units, or percentage of capacity, can be used.
2. Plot the sales value, which will be 0 at zero volume and £100,000 at £100,000 volume; link these two points with a straight line.
3. Plot variable costs, which will again be 0 at zero volume, but £60,000 at £100,000 volume of sales.
4. Note the space between the sales line and the variable cost line; this space represents the contribution, which at £100,000 sales is £40,000.
5. Plot fixed costs above variable costs; this will give a total cost line. Fixed costs, on the assumption of marginal costing, will be £25,000 at zero volume and still £25,000 at £100,000 volume. Total costs will therefore be £25,000 at zero volume and £85,000 (£25,000 + £60,000 variable cost) at £100,000 volume.

The break-even chart for X Ltd. in the coming quarter is shown at Fig. 7. This chart gives several useful pieces of information. In the first place it shows how the sales line and the total cost line intersect to give a break-even point, the point at which neither profit nor loss will be made. The chart shows this point to be at sales of £62,500. From zero to break-even sales,

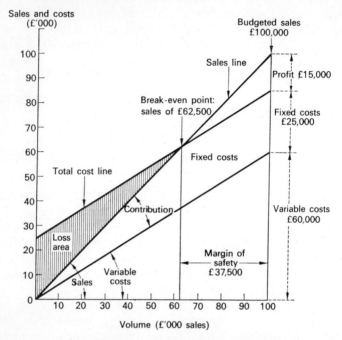

FIG. 7. Break-even chart for X Ltd. 1st quarter.

contribution increases, progressively "eating into" fixed costs until, at break-even volume, fixed costs and contribution are equal. From then on, extra contribution is net profit, since the sales line is above the total cost line. The chart also shows how contribution equals fixed cost plus profit.

Another factor which emerges from the chart is the margin of safety. This is the extent to which sales can drop before losses begin to be made. If the assumptions on costs and prices are borne out, X Ltd. can drop £37,500 below its budget sales of £100,000 before it enters the loss area, and the loss area comes into existence when sales volume is too low to yield a total contribution greater than total fixed costs.

With this chart in front of them, the managers of X Ltd. can now see what will happen if sales volume varies from the budgeted level. For example, at £80,000 sales, profit will be about £7500. They know, too, that they must sell at least 62,500 pens at £1 each to break even. Sales below that figure will not meet the fixed costs. They can see that the main determinant of break-even point is the level of fixed costs, and when the accountant mentions that he is thinking of taking on a new £1500-a-year assistant, the sales manager is quick to point out that if he does, the company will have to sell another 3750 pens if a reduction of profit is to be avoided. He worked this out by noting that the 8*s.* unit contribution must be earned 3750 times to bring in extra profit equal to the £1500 extra fixed cost.

This raises the question of the relationship between incremental sales and incremental profit. The question here is not, "What is our overall profitability on sales?", but rather "How much additional profit shall we make by selling one or more additional units?" The profit to sales ratio which X Ltd. hopes to achieve is 15% (£15,000 net profit on sales of £100,000), but the profitability of additional sales, if the company can increase sales without increasing fixed costs, is clearly much higher than this. The ratio to be considered in such cases is the ratio of contribution to sales value. This ratio ignores fixed costs and is constant at any level of sales. For X Ltd., the ratio is £40,000 to £100,000, or 40%. This ratio is known as the profit–volume ratio, since it compares additional profit (which is contribution) with additional revenue from additional volume of sales. This ratio, too, can be derived from Fig. 7.

However, it is not necessary to draw a break-even chart to find the break-even point and margin of safety. Simple formulae can give us this information, once we know sales value (S), variable costs (VC) at that level of sales, and fixed costs (FC). From these figures we can derive contribution (C), which is sales value less variable costs, or alternatively fixed costs plus net profit. Break-even point (B/E) is calculated as follows:

$$\text{Break-even point} = \text{S} \times \frac{\text{FC}}{\text{C}}.$$

$$\text{Margin of safety} = \text{S} - \text{B/E sales}.$$

$$\text{Profit–volume ratio} = \frac{\text{C}}{\text{S}} \times 100.$$

Applying these formulae to X Ltd.:

$$\text{B/E} = 100,000 \times \frac{25,000}{40,000} = \text{£}62,500.$$

$$\text{Margin of safety} = \text{£}100,000 - \text{£}62,500 = \text{£}37,500.$$

$$\text{Profit–volume ratio} = \frac{40,000}{100,000} \times 100 = 40\%.$$

We can now see what is likely to happen to the profit earned by X Ltd. in the face of uncertain demand. The executives of the company may not know exactly how many pens they will sell, but they know how far their sales can drop before they will make losses, and what extra profit they will make if sales exceed budget.

To reinforce the point, consider Y Ltd., a competitor of X Ltd., and of similar size. Y Ltd. also hopes for £100,000 worth of sales with total costs of £85,000 and a net profit of £15,000. But a marginal analysis of their costs shows that they have lower variable costs and higher fixed costs than X Ltd., which makes an interesting comparison of break-even point, margin of safety, and profit–volume ratio (Table 58).

Here is a contrasting situation for two companies operating in the same market. X Ltd., with its lower break-even point and greater margin of safety, can face a drop in sales with more equanimity than Y Ltd., whose sales can drop only £20,000 before it enters the loss area. But if the market is buoyant, Y Ltd. will be in a far stronger position to exploit it. For every extra £1 of sales, Y Ltd. will earn 15*s.* net profit, while X Ltd. will earn only 8*s.* Y Ltd., if it has planned its fixed costs wisely, should also be better prepared for expansion, with a greater capacity in its fixed cost organization and facilities than X Ltd.

TABLE 58

	Y Ltd.	X Ltd.
	£	£
Sales	100,000	100,000
Variable costs	25,000	60,000
Contribution	75,000	40,000
Fixed costs	60,000	25,000
Net profit	15,000	15,000
Break-even point	80,000	62,500
Margin of safety	20,000	37,500
Profit–volume ratio	75%	40%

Another result of fixed-variable cost structures is the factor sometimes called "leverage". Leverage is the variability of the rate of profit increase for a given increase in sales. Suppose that X Ltd. and Y Ltd. have both achieved £84,000 worth of sales. Both go on to secure a further £4000 sales, an increase of $4 \cdot 8\%$. But the increase in profit is different (Table 59).

TABLE 59. DIFFERENT LEVERAGE OF X LTD. AND Y LTD.

Company	P/V ratio	Profit at £84,000 sales	Profit from extra £4,000 sales	Profit increase
X Ltd.	40%	£8600	£1600	19%
Y Ltd.	75%	£3000	£3000	100%

In this situation Y Ltd. has a greater leverage than X Ltd., and this comes about not merely because Y Ltd. has the higher P/V ratio, but because it is operating nearer break-even point than the other company. Leverage is always greater near break-even point, as the following figures show in relation to X Ltd., alone. Assume that sales increase by £5000, (a) from £65,000 to £70,000, and (b) from £100,000 to £105,000 (Table 60).

TABLE 60. DIFFERENT LEVERAGE OF X LTD. AT DIFFERENT SALES LEVELS

	Sales to date	Profit to date	Extra profit from £5000 extra sales	Profit increase
(a)	£65,000	£1,000	£2000	200%
(b)	£100,000	£15,000	£2000	13%

The leverage at £65,000 sales, not much above break-even sales of £62,500, is far greater than at £100,000 sales. The significance of leverage is that the rate of profit increase brought about by extra sales is more a function of cost structure than of sales effort. Indeed, there could well be an inverse correlation between leverage and selling effort; as sales increase beyond break-even point, leverage will diminish, but sales effort to secure a greater hold on the market may well have to be stepped up.

Break-even analysis does, however, have certain limitations, arising mainly from the assumptions on which it rests. These assumptions ought to be clearly stated, since they will seldom be completely verified in fact. The first assumption is that fixed costs will remain fixed at a given level throughout the whole range of volume fluctuation being considered. In a short period of time, this will probably be true, but in the longer term, fixed costs must obviously rise as additional capacity is set up. Secondly, it is assumed that variable costs will increase by a constant amount per unit increase in sales volume. This, too, will tend to be the case only over a limited range of volume; as the limit of capacity is approached, variable costs per unit may well increase, because, for example, of higher material wastage, machine repairs or power costs at maximum capacity operations. Also, it is assumed that selling prices will be the same at any level of volume, whereas to get the market to absorb the maximum quantity of output it may be necessary to reduce unit prices. A further assumption concerns product mix. The examples we have used so far relate to one-product companies, but the technique is equally applicable to multi-product firms. Where, however, there are many products, and these products have different P/V ratios, the break-even chart assumes an average P/V ratio which is true only of a given proportional mix of products. The same applies to the mix of variable cost items within the total variable cost. Yet another assumption made in marginal analysis is that all fixed costs are charged against the period in which they are incurred. This is not always the case, as we saw in Chapter 3; frequently fixed manufacturing costs are added to the value of stock, and if the stocks are unsold at the end of the accounting period, the fixed cost apportioned to the stocks will be held as an asset and not written off against sales. This will not matter if stock levels remain constant. If, however, stock levels are rising, the break-even chart, by putting all fixed costs against profit, will show a lower profit than the profit and loss account, which will not include the manufacturing costs apportioned to the additional units put into stock.

Despite these assumptions, marginal analysis remains a valuable guide to managerial decisions. It is probably most useful as a short-term technique. The longer the period to which it is applied, the greater will be the volume fluctuations for which it must cater, and the less valid will be the deductions drawn from it.

It must also be noted that break-even point itself is of little practical concern to a successful and profitable business with good long-term prospects. Inside such a business, marginal analysis will be used more to highlight the incremental profitability of new opportunities than to consolidate the margin of safety between current level of business and break-even point. Only the marginal firm, hovering uncertainly between profit and loss, will focus attention on break-even point, perhaps in vain.

With these limitations in mind we can go on to look at further applications of cost–profit–volume relationships. Changes in volume have already been discussed. Forecasting the volume of sales is a marketing rather than a financial problem, and while break-even analysis cannot show what sales will be, it can at least indicate the different levels of profit likely to be earned at different levels of sales. This can be done by preparing variable budgets, i.e. budgets which show cost and revenue targets for different levels of activity, and which enable budgets to be adjusted to the actual level of activity once this is known.

The other problem areas in which marginal analysis is useful are to do with changes in price, changes in costs, and changes in product mix. The problem of fixing a price is discussed more fully in Chapter 9, but it is relevant to examine here the relationship of alternative prices to volume and profits.

X Ltd. plans at present to sell its fountain pen at 20*s*. In examining its pricing policy, the management may well like to know what the effect would be of charging, say, 18*s*. or 22*s*. Price changes will frequently have an effect on volume as well, so the management will turn again to the accountant and ask "Can you show us how, with our present cost structure, profits will be affected by given price and volume changes?" To answer their queries, the accountant will probably bring out another chart, usually called a profit–volume chart.

The profit–volume chart shows a single profit–loss line against volume of sales, taking the cost-price structure for granted. For the

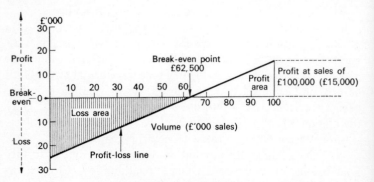

FIG. 8. Profit–volume chart.

quarterly budget figures used earlier, the profit–volume chart
will look like Fig. 8.

Like the break-even chart, the profit–volume chart shows the
level of profit at different levels of sales. But because of its
simple construction, uncomplicated by sales and cost lines, it
lends itself to graphic presentation of alternative profit structures,
based on different costs, or different prices, or both. We shall
hold costs steady and vary the prices, to produce the profit–
volume chart shown at Fig. 9. The profit and loss accounts
(Table 61) show the effect of varying the price, while costs and
number of units sold (100,000) remain constant.

TABLE 61. X LTD.

Alternative Budgets Showing Effect of Price Changes

Budget sales (units): Unit price:	100,000 18s.	100,000 20s.	100,000 22s.	100,000 24s.
	£	£	£	£
Sales	90,000	100,000	110,000	120,000
Variable costs	60,000	60,000	60,000	60,000
Contribution	30,000	40,000	50,000	60,000
Fixed costs	25,000	25,000	25,000	25,000
Net profit	5,000	15,000	25,000	35,000
B/E point	75,000	62,500	55,000	50,000
P/V ratio	33%	40%	45%	50%

While the chart at Fig. 9 shows the effect of selling 100,000
units at different prices, it also shows the profits which will result
from selling less than 100,000 units at any of these prices. If the
profit lines were continued, the charts would also show profits
at higher volumes. The chart cannot, of course, tell the sales
manager how many pens he is likely to sell at 22s., but it can tell
him that at this price sales of about £88,000 will yield the same

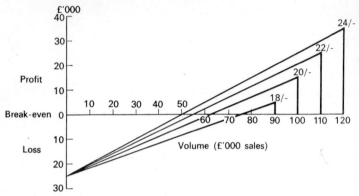

FIG. 9. Effect on profit of selling 100,000 units at different prices.

profit as £100,000 sales at 20*s*. per unit, or that if he sells at 18*s*., sales must reach about £121,000 if the company is to reach its profit target of £15,000. This sort of information can alert the sales manager to the significance of trends early in the operating period, in sufficient time for corrective action to be taken.

The next application is in the area of costs. The problem of rising costs has always been one of the biggest challenges to management. Inevitably many rising costs are passed on to customers in the form of price increases; this is the familiar inflationary spiral. Perhaps a measure of inflation is unavoidable in any developing economic community based on work specialization and commodity exchange. The problem of inflation is not that such a thing exists, but that it is liable to get out of hand if not controlled. The contribution which business managers can make to the control of inflation is largely concerned with absorbing price and wage increases rather than resorting too soon to increasing the price of their own products.

Cost reduction, however analysed, programmed, written about, talked about, and applied, is simply the result of better management, i.e. better utilization of resources. Once again, marginal analysis can offer useful information, without claiming to be a panacea.

Marginal analysis makes it clear that a business which seeks to protect its profit levels has four possible courses of action:

1. Increase unit prices, at present costs and volume.
2. Reduce total variable costs ⎱ at present prices and
3. Reduce total fixed costs   ⎰   volume.
4. Increase volume at present costs and prices.

Suppose that the management of X Ltd., having examined the budget of Table 57, considers a profit of £15,000 insufficient return on capital employed, and wants to aim instead at a net profit of £20,000. Table 62 shows how the revised budget would look under each of these four alternatives, applying them one at a time (they could of course be used in combination).

TABLE 62. X LTD.

Alternative Budgets to Raise Net Profit by £5000 to £20,000

	(1) Raise unit price to 21s.	(2) Reduce variable costs by £5000	(3) Reduce fixed costs by £5000	(4) Increase volume to £112,500 sales
Units	100,000	100,000	100,000	112,500
Price	21s.	20s.	20s.	20s.
	£	£	£	£
Sales	105,000	100,000	100,000	112,500
Variable costs	60,000	55,000	60,000	67,500
Contribution	45,000	45,000	40,000	45,000
Fixed costs	25,000	25,000	20,000	25,000
Net profit	20,000	20,000	20,000	20,000
B/E point	58,333	55,555	50,000	62,500
P/V ratio	43%	45%	40%	40%

Which of these alternatives ought X Ltd. to take? Management is the art of the possible, and no doubt the managers of X Ltd.

will do whatever they think is possible to widen the gap between costs and revenue. There are, however, some financial comments which might help towards a decision on how best to achieve the extra £5000 profit.

Increase Unit Price to 21s.

The time comes in all businesses when prices have to be increased. No firm can hold its prices steady forever. But the ability to delay price increases is a valuable contribution to the control of inflation, even though it may be a thankless task when other and less resourceful managements are not so hesitant about raising their prices. There could perhaps be times when a low price arouses suspicion, prompting prospective buyers to question quality, but in general, a circular letter announcing price increases is unwelcome to customers.

Reduce variable costs by £5000

The effect of this is to increase the amount of extra profit per extra £ of sales revenue, i.e. the profit–volume ratio, from 40% in the original budget to 45%. The break-even point also drops by about £7000 to £55,555, and this increases the margin of safety. The techniques of reducing variable costs involve product design, production engineering, method study, scrap control, purchasing, and so on. Skills of this kind are sometimes brought together in value analysis teams.

Reduce fixed costs by £5000

This has an even more pronounced effect on break-even point which drops away to £50,000. But the P/V ratio does not change, since neither sales nor variable costs are affected. Fixed costs, which are largely management and clerical costs, can be controlled by effective organization planning, office management, and O & M services.

Increase sales volume to £112,500

An increase in sales is easier said than done, but this is presumably the main task of the marketing function—to sell successfully wherever buyers can be found. Such a course will obviously not change either break-even point or P/V ratio. The extra profit is found by continuing the break-even chart at Fig. 7 (p. 158) until the gap between total costs and sales reaches £20,000.

From the financial point of view, it could be argued that the most generally beneficial alternative is No. 2, reducing variable costs. Raising prices will be unpopular with the customer and may cause a drop in volume difficult to forecast. Reducing fixed costs has the greatest effect on break-even point, but this is not a positive advantage unless the firm is operating near break-even volume; it does not improve marginal profitability. Increasing sales may be very welcome, but this involves renewed selling effort and an increased reliance on market response. Every business relies on market response, of course, but while working and waiting for this response, it may be that improvements in profitability can be brought about inside the firm. Reducing variable costs, if this can be done, brings about the greatest improvement in marginal profitability. It increases the contribution per sales £ from 8s. to 9s., which none of the other alternatives can do.

At some time or another, most firms attempt to offset rising costs by increasing the volume of sales. In such circumstances it is a great help if the marketing manager understands the incidence of costs sufficiently to ward off the feeling that the profit from his hard-won sales is being frittered away by extravagance elsewhere in the business. A firm which wants to meet rising costs with increased sales should note the extent to which the rising costs are fixed or variable. The reason for this is that, if fixed costs rise, the extra volume of sales required to offset this rise is less than if variable costs had risen by the same amount.

For example, an examination of the budget on p. 156 (Table 57) might have prompted the accountant to say: "I think our total costs will be £90,000, not £85,000." If the increased costs were

TABLE 63. X LTD.

Offsetting Increased Fixed Costs by Increased Volume

	Original budget	1st revision showing reduced profit through increased fixed costs	2nd revision, restoring profit through increased sales
	£	£	£
Sales	100,000	100,000	112,500
Variable costs	60,000	60,000	67,500
Contribution	40,000	40,000	45,000
Fixed costs	25,000	30,000	30,000
Net profit	15,000	10,000	15,000
B/E point	62,500	75,000	75,000
P/V ratio	40%	40%	40%

TABLE 64. X LTD.

Offsetting Increased Variable Costs by Increased Volume

	Original budget	1st revision, showing reduced profit through increased variable costs	2nd revision, restoring profit through increased sales
	£	£	£
Sales	100,000	100,000	114,286
Variable costs	60,000	65,000	74,286
Contribution	40,000	35,000	40,000
Fixed costs	25,000	25,000	25,000
Net profit	15,000	10,000	15,000
B/E point	62,500	71,429	71,429
P/V ratio	40%	35%	35%

all fixed costs, the required budget revision would be as Table 63 shows.

But if the increased costs were all variable costs, the required budget revision would be different (Table 64).

If the increased costs are variable costs, the sales manager has to sell 14,286 more pens in order to generate £15,000 net profit; but if the increased costs are fixed costs, he need sell only 12,500 more pens to recoup the lost profits. The reason for this is obvious when we look at the P/V ratio; as long as it is only fixed costs which are rising, each £1 of sales continues to bring in 8s. (40%) contribution. But when the variable costs rise, each £1 of sales brings in only 7s. contribution, and consequently more sales £'s are needed to yield a total extra contribution of £5000.

The rising costs forecast for a given period will often be both fixed and variable. In this situation it will be useful to separate fixed from variable cost rises, as the sales manager did in looking at the effect on profit of an increase in fixed accounting department costs.

Progress with cost reduction also needs to be measured in financial terms, and this will be explained in the next chapter. Although the marketing department is not directly responsible for production costs, an understanding of shop-floor cost control is useful to the marketing man because of the obvious effect of factory activity on customer satisfaction and profitability.

Our third problem area is that of product mix. Everything we have said so far has related to a company with only one product. Most businesses have a range of products, and this adds another dimension to policy-making. New questions arise, such as, what will it cost, and what shall we gain from starting a new line? Should we discontinue one of our present lines? Which products are most profitable?

W Ltd. also makes and sells fountain pens in competition with X Ltd. and Y Ltd. But W Ltd. manufactures three products, P.10, P.20 and P.30, all of which sell at 20s. each. Let us assume that W Ltd. has the same total budget as X Ltd. Obviously, the management is not content to work with total cost and profit figures; it wants to know how much cost each product incurs and how much profit it makes. An analysis of the budget is therefore produced. This analysis attempts the traditional task of ensuring that each product bears its fair share of all company costs. Fixed costs are therefore allocated or apportioned to the three products, and this leads to a net profit figure for each (Table 65).

TABLE 65. W LTD.

Analysed Budget Profit and Loss Account, 1st Quarter

	Total	P.10	P.20	P.30
	£	£	£	£
Sales	100,000	50,000	20,000	30,000
Variable costs	60,000	36,000	8,000	16,000
Contribution	40,000	14,000	12,000	14,000
Fixed costs	25,000	14,500	8,000	2,500
Net profit/loss[a]	15,000	500[a]	4,000	11,500
Net profit to sales	15%	1%[a]	20%	38%

Several conclusions might be drawn from this analysed budget. P.30, for example, has the highest ratio of net profit to sales, and is far and away the most profitable product. P.10 is making a small loss, but with increased volume it could presumably be made to break even. Perhaps the company should try to sell more of P.10 and P.30, if necessary at the expense of P.20.

These conclusions are misleading, and the trouble lies in the allocation and apportionment of fixed costs. This procedure has a venerable history, but its origin and use is concerned mainly with decisions on *a fair price for work done*, where price is, by agreement, based mainly on the costs of carrying out the work. The costs of executing an order or contract are largely the direct costs, but clearly each contract benefits from the general overhead facilities (management, general purpose plant, office services, etc.) the cost of which must be met from total contract revenue. Consequently when prices are based on costs, fixed overheads must be parcelled out to the individual contracts, orders or products.

This reasoning is valid, but is irrelevant to the budget situation in which we have placed W Ltd. Here, the problem is not one of justifying a cost-plus price. The problem is to find a sales mix which will optimize the marginal income (i.e. the additional profit) to be earned in a given period, *given an existing price-structure not dependent on the supplier's costs*. In this situation, fixed costs should not be apportioned to products, and for two main reasons:

1. The basis of apportionment is frequently arbitrary.
2. Fixed costs, whether apportioned or not, are irrelevant to short-term volume problems, because they are assumed to be unaffected by changes in the level or type of output.

The difficulty of accurately attributing a fair share of fixed costs to individual contracts or products is immense. It is true that some items of fixed cost can be wholly identified with a specific product; for example, the foreman in charge of P.10 production, being on the staff, may receive a fixed salary of £1200 p.a., which is £400 per quarter. This £400 can be accurately allocated to P.10. But there are many common costs which cannot be identified with individual products, and these have to be apportioned on whatever basis seems reasonable. Factory rent, for example, can be apportioned to the three products in proportion to the amount of floor space each occupies. But how can you apportion the managing director's salary or market research costs? Or invoicing costs, if most invoices refer to all three products?

Costing textbooks can produce intricate and ingenious answers to these questions, but to no purpose in our present line of inquiry. There is no point in doing well that which does not need to be done at all.

Since the fixed costs will by definition remain fixed whatever the volume or type of output, we can simply ignore them when planning an optimum product mix. The profit figure we should really be looking at is, of course, the profit–volume ratio, and a more useful analysis of the budget profit and loss account would be as Table 66 shows.

TABLE 66. W LTD.

Analysed Budget Profit and Loss Account, 1st Quarter

	Total	P.10	P.20	P.30
% of total sales	100%	50%	20%	30%
	£	£	£	£
Sales	100,000	50,000	20,000	30,000
Variable costs	60,000	36,000	8,000	16,000
Contribution	40,000	14,000	12,000	14,000
Fixed costs	25,000			
Net profit	15,000			
P/V ratio	40% (average for this mix)	28%	60%	47%

This analysis tells the management of W Ltd. that sales of P.10 yield 28% contribution (5s. 5d. in the sales £) sales of P.20 yield 60% contribution (12s. in the £), and P.30 sales, yield a contribution of 47% (9s. 5d. in the £). On average, sales in the budgeted mix will produce an overall P/V ratio of 40%, but a different mix will produce a different average rate of contribution. The question to be decided is, "What achievable mix will optimize the contribution?" The optimum contribution is not necessarily the largest; there is always the need to balance marketing and production resources in both the short and longer term against the obvious attractions of maximum profit in the immediate future.

These problems are total business problems, not simply financial ones. The sales manager in particular must be listened to when alternative product strategies are being discussed. What would happen, for example, if W Ltd. discontinued P.10 and P.30, putting all its production and selling effort into P.20? Theoretically, £100,000 sales of P.20 would yield a contribution of £60,000 and a net profit of £45,000. But will the market take P.20 in such large quantities? Will customers deal with W Ltd., so readily if they are not offered the full range of products? Is the less profitable but more popular P.10 a lead-in for sales of P.20?

Problems of this kind can be answered only by people in touch with buying trends, customer preferences, and market opportunities. The financial analyst as such has no expertise in this area; he simply hopes that when production and sales expansion is being planned, the financial implications of alternative courses of action will be borne in mind.

An optimum budget could be constructed mathematically, if the availability of all resources and the response of the market could be predicted to an acceptable degree of probability. In practice, some unsophisticated trial-and-error may give sufficient

TABLE 67. W LTD.

Analysed Budget Profit and Loss Account, 1st Quarter, showing Revised Sales Mix

	Total	P.10	P.20	P.30
% of total sales	100%	30%	50%	20%
	£	£	£	£
Sales	100,000	30,000	50,000	20,000
Variable costs	52,200	21,600	20,000	10,600
Contribution	47,800	8,400	30,000	9,400
Fixed costs	25,000	———	———	———
Net profit	22,800			
P/V ratio	48% (average for this mix)	28%	60%	47%
Net profit to sales	23%			

guidance. If, for example, W Ltd., decided to concentrate sales on P.20, it might adopt the budget shown in Table 67.

The effect of this alternative mix on break-even point should also be noted. The first mix, in Table 65 produces the same break-even point as the X Ltd. budget in Table 58, namely £62,500. But the break-even point in the revised mix budget is different (Table 68).

TABLE 68. W LTD.

Comparison of Break-even Points for Alternative Sales Mixes

	Mix 1	Mix 2
	%	%
	P.10 50	P.10 30
	P.20 20	P.20 50
	P.30 30	P.30 20
	£	£
Sales	100,000	100,000
Fixed costs	25,000	25,000
Contribution	40,000	47,800
B/E point:	$£100,000 \times \dfrac{25,000}{40,000}$	$£100,000 \times \dfrac{25,000}{47,800}$
	= £62,500	= £52,200

The point could be further emphasized by drawing break-even charts for budgeted operations at each mix. The chart for Mix 1 of Table 68 would be the same as that in Fig. 7. Mix 2 would produce a chart with a wider contribution angle, i.e. a wider angle between the sales line and the variable cost line. The effect of the more profitable mix is in fact to reduce total variable costs, and indicates a more profitable application of resources.

It should be noted that a break-even chart can be constructed only for a business *as a whole*. One of the dangers of the cost analysis shown in Table 65 is that it tempts people to draw break-even charts for individual products. The validity of a break-even chart for individual products would depend on the accuracy of the fixed cost apportionment, and such a chart would be useful only if each product incurred all its costs independently of the other products. This would virtually make each product a business on its own.

Before W Ltd. could embark on the sales programme reflected in the Mix 2 budget, the production manager would have to check that in fact he had available the necessary resources to switch production to P.20. It might be found that during the coming quarter there were limitations on materials, labour, machine-hours, etc., which could restrict the supply of products as required by the proposed sales budget. In such a situation, a further index to guide product policy would be the contribution per unit of limiting factor.

If there were a limitation on supplies of a basic raw material, the following schedule would bring out the relevant factors (Table 69).

TABLE 69.

	Total	P.10	P.20	P.30
	£	£	£	£
Raw material cost per unit	—	0·33	0·30	0·17
Raw material needed, Mix 2	28,000	10,000	15,000	3,000
Contribution (Table 65)	47,800	8,400	30,000	9,400
Contribution per £ of raw material	—	0·84	2·00	3·13

The first question for W Ltd. is, have we £28,000 worth of raw material available? If so, this may be sufficient reassurance that the proposed budget can be adopted. But even if W Ltd. has the required material available, it is still worth remembering that £1 of raw material invested in P.30 will bring in £3·13 in contribution, as against £2·00 for P.20 and £0·84 for P.10. If there were no other limitations, either of customer demand, finance, or production capacity, W Ltd. could in theory maximize its profit in the coming quarter by concentrating solely on P.30. Assuming that there was no more than £28,000 of raw material available, production and sale of P.30 only would yield a contribution of £28,000 × 3·13, or £87,640. If all the material were used on P.20, the contribution would be only £28,000 × 2·00, or £56,000.

Whatever the mix finally decided, the management of W Ltd., while recognizing that the budgeted mix is unlikely to be exactly achieved, will at least have a yardstick to measure whether, and by how much, the actual mix is more or less profitable than the budgeted mix. These and other yardsticks for measuring actual performance will be described in detail in the next chapter.

Summary

Uncertainty about future demand, rising costs, changing product policies, and technological developments are all part of the climate of change in which a business must either thrive or decline. Managerial plans and budgets must therefore be flexible if they are to be useful.

Marginal analysis is a useful extension of business forecasting and budgeting. It focuses attention on the way in which profits will be affected by changes in costs, prices, and volume of business. It does this mainly by distinguishing between fixed and variable costs.

Fixed costs are costs which are not expected to vary as a direct result of changes in the volume of goods sold. Variable costs are those which do vary in proportion to changes in the volume of sales. Many items of cost are partly fixed and partly variable. Recognition of the fixed and variable elements of cost is not always easy but is a help in reaching managerial decisions on budgeting, profit planning, marketing, and cost control.

Break-even point and margin of safety indicate the extent to which a business can sustain a drop in sales without actually making a loss. Profit–volume ratios, particularly in multi-product companies, can usefully indicate the additional profit made on additional sales, provided there is no increase in fixed costs. This shows the effect of product mix on profit more clearly than net profit per unit based on total unit costs.

The need for cost control action and the way in which cost control should be applied is more clearly understood when the fixed or variable nature of rising costs is recognized.

CHAPTER 8

Measuring Progress

THE financial progress made by a business reflects the progress it has made in achieving customer satisfaction. Customer satisfaction is achieved by offering for sale goods or services which customers are willing and able to buy, and supplying the goods and services in the manner agreed.

Financial progress is measured in terms of profit. Profit, as we saw in the last chapter, results from the interaction of prices, costs, and volume of business. Consequently, progress towards profits will be measurable to the extent that actual prices, costs, and volumes approach planned prices, costs, and volumes. To give operating managers and their staffs some interim measure of how well they are doing profitwise, the company and departmental budgets are developed into financial standards of achievement which can be used as guides to operating decisions and actions.

In Chapter 2 the business cycle was explained as the process whereby raw material became finished goods which created debtors when transferred on credit to customers and brought cash back into the business when the debtors cleared their accounts. This was the process which generated profit. The amounts involved at each stage of the cycle are carefully planned, and standards are set to ensure that financial values are carefully preserved throughout this cycle of current asset transformation.

For marketing people, these financial standards will be expressed as sales quotas, advertising appropriations, sales office budgets, selling expense budgets, and so on. We noted in Chapter

6 that selling expenses cannot be engineered like direct costs. All the same, field salesmen can be encouraged to set themselves targets or standards of expense related to the journeys they make, the goodwill they create, and ultimately the orders they get. Perhaps the operative phrase is, "set themselves targets". An imposed standard does not motivate people in the right direction for very long. Whatever standards are adopted, they are unlikely to be achieved unless those responsible for financial performance are committed to the standard, and commitment is unlikely without some two-way discussion of the reasonableness of the proposed revenue and cost levels.

Acceptance of a standard will create a spontaneous awareness of whether or not the standard has been reached. In other words, a standard of performance will create awareness of a variance, which will in turn show the need for corrective action.

The explanation of standards and variances given in this chapter will add financial detail to the general concept of control as described in Chapter 1. We shall pay particular attention to the standards and variances which concern marketing people. But standards and variances related to production will also be described, since factory output is what the marketing man attempts to market, and an understanding of production costs and problems is essential for anyone working explicitly towards customer satisfaction.

Standard costs are predetermined costs, i.e. costs on which an acceptable limit has been placed in advance. Variances are the amounts by which actual costs differ from standard costs. Standard costs answer the question, "What costs ought we to incur in making and selling this product, in relation to the prices we charge and the level of sales we hope for?" Variances answer the question, "What was the difference between planned and actual sales levels, prices and costs?" These differences can be analysed by retracing the steps which led to the original standard costs and budgets. This will test the value of the original standard, which lies in the significance of the variances it discloses. The significance of variances is that they focus attention on the areas where plans and progress are out of balance and which call for corrective action, either to performance or to plan.

Standards and variances can best be described by illustration. Suppose that you own and run Industrial Units Ltd., a small business turning out wooden units for industrial use. There are five men working in the plant, plus a few others on supervision and office work. You supply three models, type A, type B, and type C. Each is made up from one standard size of wood, which you buy for 1s. a foot. Type A requires 40 ft of wood, type B needs 20 ft, and type C 60 ft.

Your five men work a 40-hour week and you pay them 10s. per hour. By the manufacturing methods agreed and adopted by the labour force, a type A model takes 6 hours to construct, a type B takes 4 hours and a type C 8 hours. The labour force provides a factory capacity of 200 direct labour hours per week.

All costs apart from direct material and labour are assumed to be fixed costs in the short period. These costs, covering supervision, office costs, rent of premises, selling costs, and miscellaneous items, are reckoned to come to £50 per week.

You spend most of your time outside getting orders. Current contracts have enabled you to stabilize weekly production and delivery at the following rate:

Type A, 20 units.
Type B, 10 units.
Type C, 5 units.

Your price list is as follows: type A, £8 each; type B, £5; type C, £12.

From the information given above, your accountant can prepare some standards and budgets. Unit standard costs were prepared on the full costing basis traditional in British industry, and were worked out as shown in Table 70.

Fixed overhead can be apportioned to production at a standard rate per direct labour hour, and this is the basis of apportionment used here. Five men each working 40 hours per week provide a plant capacity of 200 labour hours, and since fixed costs are

TABLE 70. INDUSTRIAL UNITS LTD.

Unit Standard Costs and Prices

Type A	£
Direct material (40 ft at 1*s*. per ft)	2·0
Direct labour (6 hr at 10*s*. per hr)	3·0
Fixed overhead (apportioned: see below)	1·5
Total unit cost	6·5
Selling price	8·0
Standard net profit per unit	1·5

Type B	
Direct material (20 ft at 1*s*. per ft)	1·0
Direct labour (4 hr at 10*s*. per hr)	2·0
Fixed overhead (4 hr at 5*s*. per hr)	1·0
Total unit cost	4·0
Selling price	5·0
Standard net profit per unit	1·0

Type C	
Direct material (60 ft at 1*s*. per ft)	3·0
Direct labour (8 hr at 10*s*. per hr)	4·0
Fixed overhead (8 hr at 5*s*. per hr)	2·0
Total unit cost	9·0
Selling price	12·0
Standard net profit per unit	3·0

budgeted at £50, the overhead rate per labour hour will be £(50 ÷ 200) or 5*s*. This rate, applied to the standard number of hours required to produce one unit of each type, gives the amount of fixed overhead which each unit of production must absorb when produced and will recover when sold.

From the marginal point of view, this parcelling out of theoretical fractions of fixed cost looks like figure-juggling of a not very helpful kind. What full costing does, however, is to apply to unit contribution the fixed cost to profit ratio found in the total contribution at budgeted volume of sales. For example, a business earning a total contribution of £100 would gain £40 net profit if fixed costs were £60. If unit contribution were 20*s.* and 100 units were sold, each unit could be said to have provided 8*s.* towards fixed costs and 12*s.* towards net profit. If no more than 80 units were sold, the relationship between volume, fixed cost, and net profit could be expressed in one of three ways:

(a) Each of 80 units has provided 15*s.* towards total fixed costs (£60) and 5*s.* towards total net profit (£20). This is the actual, or historical approach, and is of little use in business planning since the volume of sales can seldom be known in advance.

(b) Each of 80 units has provided 20*s.* of contribution, which it was bound to do at any volume, given the cost/price structure; total fixed costs absorb £60 of the £80 total contribution, leaving £20 total net profit. This is the marginal approach, which gives the message "Contribution is down by £20, so you have lost £20 net profit".

(c) Each of 80 units has provided standard amounts of 8*s.* towards net profit and 12*s.* towards fixed costs. This gives in total £32 towards net profit and £48 towards fixed costs. However, fixed costs are £60, which the standard fixed cost recovery rate can provide only if 100 units are sold. In fact, 20 fewer units than this were sold. Therefore fixed costs were under-recovered by (20 × 12*s.*) or £12; this under-recovery can be met only from the total standard net profit amount of £32, which must provide the £12 of under-recovered fixed overhead, and will drop to £20. This is the standard full (or total) costing approach, which gives the message "You have had to transfer £12 out of standard profit to cover fixed costs".

The standard full costing approach may seem long-winded, but it is the one almost universally adopted by UK firms with any standard costing system at all. It differs from the marginal approach in that it apportions fixed cost to units of product, and this can be useful if it helps management and workers to question and maximize the benefits which should accompany these costs. Because the full costing approach is so widespread, we shall use it in the example worked out in this chapter.

Standard costs for direct cost items can genuinely be attributed to individual units of product. Direct materials and direct labour are the most obvious of these. All overheads can be seen as enabling costs, the costs of borrowed capital, research, management, information, plant and tools, energy, lubricants, services of all kinds, and, of course, marketing, which provide the conditions in which direct labour can work productively on direct materials. Product design and work methods, plus agreed raw material costs and wage rates, give the accountant the information he needs to prepare standard costs.

Notice, however, that it is not the accountant who sets the standards. This is done by marketing, production, technical, and administrative managers. Production engineering establishes methods and operation sequence; time-study measures the length of time needed to complete a job; purchasing skill secures the materials at a good price; union negotiations determine wage rates; inspection checks quality and insists where necessary on either scrap or re-work costs. Managerial decisions in all these areas play a large part in setting cost standards, but in two crucial areas the decisions lie elsewhere. As we have already noted, decisions on how fast to buy lie with customers, and decisions on how fast to produce lie ultimately with production workers.

Industrial and commercial variables like these are the background to standard costs. Before the accountant can prepare useful standard costs, some agreement on time, quantity, and quality standards of performance is essential; agreement between the firm and its customers, and, inside the firm, agreement between all who co-operate in attempting to satisfy the customers.

As a result of such agreement, your accountant in Industrial Units Ltd. has been able to prepare the standard costs set out in Table 70. Many industrial firms have complex products which require intricate standard cost calculations, but the principles are always the same: the direct cost of each productive operation

TABLE 71. INDUSTRIAL UNITS LTD.
Weekly Sales and Production Budget

	Type A		Type B		Type C		Total
	Unit	Total qty.	Unit	Total qty.	Unit	Total qty.	
Quantity		20		10		5	35
Standard hours required per unit		6		4		8	—
Total		120		40		40	200
	£	£	£	£	£	£	£
Direct material	2·0	40	1·0	10	3·0	15	65
Direct labour	3·0	60	2·0	20	4·0	20	100
Fixed overhead	1·5	30	1·0	10	2·0	10	50
Total standard cost	6·5	130	4·0	40	9·0	45	215
Sales value	8·0	160	5·0	50	12·0	60	270
Standard profit	1·5	30	1·0	10	3·0	15	55

is the cost of one unit of input (hours of work or physical quantities of material) multiplied by the number of input units called for to complete the job. To this will be added variable overhead in appropriate amounts (though for simplicity this was omitted from the examples given), and finally, there may be an apportionment of fixed costs, depending on whether the full or marginal costing approach is preferred.

Armed with the standard costs shown in Table 70 and your own sales estimates, your accountant can draw up a budget. Again, for simplicity, we shall take a budget period of one week and assume that there are no stocks carried over from one period to the next (Table 71).

The figures in Table 71 show that if you sell 35 units in the budgeted mix and at budgeted costs and prices, you will make £55 profit.

In one particular week (call it week 1), only four men were available for work. Because of the urgent need to meet delivery promises they agreed to work longer hours than usual, and you offered them 11s. per hour as a production bonus. Between them they produced 16 units of type A, 18 of type B, and 8 of type C.

TABLE 72. INDUSTRIAL UNITS LTD.
Budget/Actual Comparison: Week 1

Actual		Original budget
	£	£
Direct material (1680 ft at 1s. 1d. per ft)	91	65
Direct labour (220 hr at 11s. per hr)	121	100
Fixed overhead	52	50
Total costs	264	215
Sales value (16 at £9; 18 at £4; 8 at £11)	304	270
Net profit	40	55
Total profit variance	£15	

G*

They each put in 55 hours, and used 1680 ft of wood. This week the wood cost 1*s.* 1*d.* per foot. Fixed costs amounted to £52 because of unexpected increases in expenditure on certain items. Selling prices on dispatches were also modified: type A sold for £9, type B for £4, and type C for £11. How much profit did you make? (See Table 72.)

The knowledge that your expected profit of £55 has shrunk to £40 prompts you to ask how this has come about, and a set of variances can be prepared to analyse the total variance into its component parts. It must be stressed from the start, however, that variance analysis does not tell you why actual achievement is different from planned achievement. Like the ratio analysis described in Chapter 4, it suggests problem areas that need investigation.

Profit is the difference between costs and revenue. A profit variance will therefore be analysed into sales variances and cost variances (Table 73).

TABLE 73. INDUSTRIAL UNITS LTD.

Summary of Cost, Sales, and Profit Variances

	Original budget	Actual	Variance
	£	£	£
Sales	270	304	34 (F)
Costs	215	264	49 (A)
Profit	£55	£40	£15 (A)

(A) = Adverse variance, reducing profit.
(F) = Favourable variance, increasing profit.

A variance is said to be adverse if, taken by itself, it reduces profit, and is favourable if it increases profit. Profit grows when the gap between sales and costs widens; adverse variances (lower sales, high costs) are those which narrow this gap, and favourable variances (higher sales, lower costs) are those which widen the gap. The terminology is not ideal, since higher costs wisely incurred may well stimulate even higher sales or lower costs elsewhere in the business, either way tending to increase profit. But use of the symbols (A) and (F) does at least avoid plus and minus signs, which can be confusing.

First, the sales variances. Why were sales £34 above budget? There are two main variables: volume and price, but in a multi-product business like this, volume can be further split into quantity and mix. Budgeted quantity was 35 units, but you actually sold 42. Secondly, you sold this 42 in a proportional mix of types A, B, and C different from the proportional mix assumed in the budget. Thirdly, actual selling prices were different from budgeted prices. How much of the total sales variance of £34 can be ascribed to each of these variables?

The sales quantity variance arises as follows. The budget assumed that 35 units would sell for £270 (see Table 71); 42 units were actually sold. If sales quantity alone had changed, leaving mix and price as budgeted, the sales revenue would have increased in the same proportion as the total quantity, i.e. by 20%. This would have meant sales of £324 and a sales quantity variance of £54 (F).

Sales mix, however, did vary. The budget mix was: 57% of total quantity in type A, 29% in type B, 14% in type C. The actual mix was: 38% type A, 43% type B, 19% type C. Sales of the actual quantity at the actual mix, but at budget prices, would have been:

			£
Type A	16 at	£8	128
Type B	18 at	£5	90
Type C	8 at	£12	96
			£314

The effect of the mix variance is to reduce the sales revenue from £324 to £314, which means an adverse sales mix variance of £10.

The third variable was price. The actual mix was sold at prices differing from those in the budget, and the result was:

			£
Type A	16 at	£9	144
Type B	18 at	£4	72
Type C	8 at	£11	88
			£304

The price differences have caused a further net drop of £10 in sales revenue, which involves an adverse sales price variance. The sales variances can be summarized as Table 74.

TABLE 74

	£	£
Budgeted sales		270
Sales quantity variance	54 (F)	
Sales mix variance	10 (A)	
Sales price variance	10 (A)	
Total sales variance	——	34 (F)
Actual sales		304

What sort of action do these sales variances suggest?

The general "message" of these sales variance is that the sales function is responsible for securing revenue or turnover. We shall see later that the provision of contribution is a more positive financial target for the sales force, but for the moment we are working along traditional lines.

The sales quantity variance arises because the quantity of units sold is different from the budgeted quantity. Sale of an extra 7 units, disregarding mix and price changes, would bring an extra £54 in sales. The budget has been more than achieved, and the action called for in such cases is not so much corrective action as an investigation to see whether the increase can be sustained. If the market is larger than was supposed, sales plans can be revised upwards.

The message of the sales mix variance is that the proportionate mix of the quantity sold brings in £10 less turnover than the budgeted mix would have done, and that this trend needs to be reversed if a budgeted turnover proportionate to the number of units sold is to be achieved. So the message is "Sell more of type A, ease back on type B and to a lesser extent on type C". How far customers will respond to a redirection of sales effort, and how far this week's quantity and mix differences indicate production rather than selling problems, is a matter for further investigation.

However, the sales price variance is certainly not a production matter. Discretion to vary prices lies with top management, and in your Industrial Units company this means you of course. Whatever reasons prompted you to seek or accept price changes, their net effect was to reduce turnover by a further £10. Leaving the actual pricing decisions on one side for the moment, the action called for here is to look at the effect of the price changes on future volume, to decide whether the revised prices are permanent or temporary, and to review the future sales quantity and mix which will be necessary to secure the required turnover. In practice, short-term price manipulation is secured by means of temporary discounts, which are essentially price variances.

The sales variances have shown the difference between budgeted and actual sales quantities, and because delivery is from the shop floor rather than the warehouse, the same quantity and mix changes will affect production. It is obvious that we cannot directly compare actual production costs with production costs in the original budget, which were computed in respect of different quantities of output. Comparison of original budgeted costs with actual costs must therefore be done in two stages: (a) apply unit standard costs to the actual quantity produced, and (b) compare standard cost of actual quantity produced with actual cost of actual quantity produced. The figures appropriate to each stage are as shown in Table 75.

TABLE 75. INDUSTRIAL UNITS LTD.

Stages in the Measurement and Control of Costs: Week 1

	£	
Standard cost of budgeted quantity and mix	215	(Table 71)
Standard cost of actual quantity and mix	248	(Table 76)
Actual cost of actual quantity and mix	264	(Table 72)

The standard cost of actual quantity and mix is called an adjusted budget. The assumption is that had you been able to foresee exactly the quantity and mix you would make and sell, you would have done so, and would not have set your sights on a target profit of £55. The difference between standard cost of budgeted production and standard cost of actual production is an adjustment which must be taken into account in attempting to explain why only £40 profit was made instead of the £55 budgeted profit. In a standard full costing system, the adjusted budget will be the aggregate of the full unit standard costs of each unit actually sold. In calculating the adjusted budget, the fixed cost apportioned to each unit will be treated arithmetically in the same way as variable cost, leaving over- or under-recovery to be dealt with in the second stage. In our example the total standard cost adjustment is £33, and being an increase in cost is an adverse variance. The corresponding sales value adjustment is £44 (quantity and mix variances only). The adjustment to the original budget is calculated as Table 76 shows.

Notice that the basis of adjustment is volume alone. This is why only the sales volume variance of £44 (sales quantity plus sales mix variances) is included in the adjustment, which leads to a revised budget still based on standard costs and standard selling prices.

Notice also the reference to standard hours produced. One standard hour is said to be produced when a direct worker produces an article manufacture of which is reckoned to need 1 hour's work at the standard pace. The standard time for this job will thus be 1 hour, regardless of the length of time actually taken to produce it. Total standard hours produced can be compared

TABLE 76. INDUSTRIAL UNITS LTD.

Adjustment of Budget from Budget Volume to Actual Volume: Week 1

	Adjusted budget							Original budget	Adjustment
	Type A		Type B		Type C		Total		
	Unit	Total qty.	Unit	Total qty.	Unit	Total qty.			
Quantity	16		18		8		42	35	7
Standard hours produced per unit	6		4		8			200	32
Total		96		72		64	232		
	£	£	£	£	£	£	£	£	£
Direct material	2·0	32	1·0	18	3·0	24	74	65	9
Direct labour	3·0	48	2·0	36	4·0	32	116	100	16
Fixed overhead	1·5	24	1·0	18	2·0	16	58	50	8
Total standard cost	6·5	104	4·0	72	9·0	72	248	215	33
Sales value (standard)	8·0	128	5·0	90	12·0	96	314	270	44
Standard profit	1·5	24	1·0	18	3·0	24	66	55	11

with total hours actually worked to give a general indication of efficiency.

The differences between the adjusted budget items and the actual cost and revenue items arise mainly because of income and expenditure differences, but in a full costing system there will also be fixed cost recovery differences. All these differences total £26, the net result of a decrease in sales value (adverse price variance £10) and an increase in cost (adverse expenditure and recovery variances £16, to be explained below) (Table 77).

TABLE 77. INDUSTRIAL UNITS LTD.
Variance Summary: Week 1

	£	£
Standard profit (budgeted volume)		55
Volume adjustment:		
Sales volume	44 (F)	
Cost	33 (A)	
Profit	———	11 (F)
Standard profit (actual volume)		66
Cost and revenue variances:		
Sales price	10 (A)	
Cost	16 (A)	
Profit	———	26 (A)
Actual profit		£40

The sales variances have already been explained, and all that remains is to analyse the £16 adverse cost variances. These variances arise from a comparison of the adjusted budget and the actual operating results. As far as internal management is concerned, these are the variances most relevant to day-to-day financial control, since (apart from the fixed cost recovery complication) the adjusted budget shows the acceptable limit of expenditure appropriate to the actual level of activity. The operating summary showing the adjusted budget/actual comparison is as Table 78 shows.

TABLE 78. INDUSTRIAL UNITS LTD.

Operating Summary: Week 1

Item	Adjusted budget (Table 76)	Actual (Table 72)	Variance
	£	£	£
Direct material	74	91	17 (A)
Direct labour	116	121	5 (A)
Fixed overhead	58	52	6 (F)
Total costs	248	264	16 (A)
Sales value	314	304	10 (A)
Net profit	£66	£40	£26 (A)

The cost variances arise because production staff have acted differently from the way in which it was assumed that they would act, given a certain programme of work and certain productive resources. These differences have already been summarized in the budget comparison statement of Table 72. Now we shall analyse them more closely, taking each variable one by one.

The most common production cost variances are the following, all but one of which is illustrated in our example:

> Materials price variance.
> Materials usage variance.
> Labour rate variance.
> Labour efficiency variance.
> Variable overhead expenditure variance.
> Fixed overhead recovery variance.
> Fixed overhead expenditure variance.

Materials price variance

This arises because the actual purchase price of materials is different from the budgeted purchase price. The price difference is applied to the actual quantity of materials used, since the price increase has to be paid on all materials bought and used.

Formula:

(Standard price less actual price) × actual quantity
= (1s. − 1s. 1d.) × 1680
= 1d. (A) × 1680
= £7 (A)

Materials usage variance

This arises because the actual quantity of material used is different from the standard quantity specified for the actual volume of production. The quantity difference is costed at the standard price, the price variance having been eliminated.

Formula:

(Standard quantity less actual quantity) × standard price
= (1480 − 1680) × 1s.
= 200 (A) × 1s.
= £10 (A)

The two materials variances total £17 (A), which is the difference shown in the operating summary of Table 78.

Labour rate variance

This arises because the actual labour rate is different from the budgeted labour rate. The rate difference is applied to the total number of hours actually worked.

Formula:

(Standard rate less actual rate) × actual hours worked
= (10s. − 11s.) × 220
= 1s. (A) × 220
= £11 (A)

Labour efficiency variance

This arises because the actual hours worked are different from the standard hours produced. This variance is sometimes called labour time variance. The difference in hours worked and standard hours produced is costed at the standard rate, the rate variance having been eliminated.

Formula:

(Standard hours produced less actual hours worked) × standard rate

= (232 − 220) × 10*s*.

= 12 (F) × 10*s*.

= £6 (F)

The two labour variances total £5 (A), which is the difference shown in the operating summary (Table 78).

Variable overhead expenditure variance

This arises because actual variable overhead expenditure is different from the standard variable overhead expenditure appropriate to the adjusted budget, i.e. the actual level of production. This variance was not included in the example. In theory, separate quantity and rate variances could be calculated in respect of each item of variable cost—consumable stores, power, etc.—but in practice little benefit is derived from the high clerical cost of calculating all these variances as a matter of routine.

Fixed overhead recovery variances

This arises because the actual volume (or level of activity) is different from the budgeted volume to which total fixed costs were apportioned in calculating the unit overhead rate. The higher the volume, the lower the average fixed cost per unit for a given level of total fixed cost. But if the average fixed cost per unit is determined in advance and apportioned at a standard rate to each unit of activity, any difference between budgeted and actual volume will cause either over-recovery or under-recovery of fixed overhead. The unit of activity most frequently used is the direct labour hour, and the fixed overhead volume variance arises because the number of standard hours actually produced (see Table 76) is different from the standard hours required and allowed in the original budget.

Formula:

(Standard hours produced less budgeted hours required) × standard fixed overhead rate
= [232 (Table 76) − 200 (Table 71)] × £0·25 (Table 70)
= 32 (F) × £0·25
= £8 (A)

The original budget figure for labour hours required is used, and not the adjusted budget figure. This is because the standard recovery rate was of necessity based on the original budgeted figure, which must therefore be used as the yardstick with which to measure the variance.

The fixed overhead volume variance can be further analysed to show the two main factors causing the difference between budgeted hours required and standard hours produced. These two factors are capacity and efficiency.

Fixed overhead capacity variance

This arises because the number of direct labour hours actually worked is different from the number of direct labour hours required in the original budget and which we recognized as being the capacity of the production unit (see p. 182).

Formula:

(Hours actually worked less budgeted hours required) × standard fixed overhead rate
= [220 (Table 72) − 200 (Table 71)] × £0·25
= 20 (F) × £0·25
= £5 (F)

Fixed overhead efficiency variance

This arises because the number of direct labour hours actually worked is different from the standard hours produced, i.e. the number of direct labour hours which should have been taken had the work been carried out at the standard pace.

Formula:

(Standard hours produced less hours actually worked) × standard fixed overhead rate

= [232 (Table 76) — 220 (Table 72)] × £0·25

= 12 (F) × £0·25

= £3 (F)

It can now be seen how the fixed overhead volume variance equals the sum of the fixed overhead capacity and efficiency variances:

Volume = Capacity + Efficiency variances
£8 (F) = £5 (F)   + £3 (F)

The analysis of the volume variance into capacity and efficiency components is useful because it adds to managerial awareness of what is going on in the production department. It is not difficult to visualize a situation in which there is no volume variance, but a lack of capacity is made up for by a gain in efficiency. If the four men had worked only 40 hours each during the week, there would have been a capacity loss of 40 hours. If they had produced output worth 200 standard hours (which they would do by an efficiency gain) there would have been no fixed overhead volume variance, but this would not have meant that fixed overhead recovery was proceeding according to budget. The fixed cost recovery variances would in this case have been: capacity £10 (A); efficiency £10 (F); volume 0.

Fixed overhead expenditure variance

This arises because actual fixed overhead expenditure is different from the budgeted fixed overhead expenditure. The expected level

H

of fixed overhead expenditure is, of course, the same in both the original and the adjusted budgets.

Formula:

Budgeted fixed overhead expenditure less actual fixed overhead expenditure

= £50 − £52

= £2 (A)

We can now compile a complete variance summary (Table 79).

TABLE 79. INDUSTRIAL UNITS LTD.

Variance Summary, Week 1, Based on Full Costing

	£	£	
Original budgeted profit		55	
Actual profit		40	
Total profit variance		15 (A)	
			(Table 73)
Sales value variances:			
Quantity	54 (F)		
Mix	10 (A)		
Price	10 (A)		
		34 (F)	(Table 74)
Standard cost variances:			
Budget adjustment		33 (A)	(Table 76)
Materials price	7 (A)		
Materials usage	10 (A)		
		17 (A)	(Table 78)
Labour rate	11 (A)		
Labour efficiency	6 (F)		
		5 (A)	(Table 78)
Fixed overhead recovery = capacity	5 (F)		
Fixed overhead recovery = efficiency	3 (F)		
Fixed overhead expenditure	2 (A)		
		6 (F)	(Table 78)
Total profit variance		£15 (A)	(Table 72)

A statement like this is a useful document in the hands of the manager of a business. If you were running Industrial Units Ltd., you would want some indication of the reasons why your expected profit of £55 dropped to £40. With variance analysis you have this indication; without it, you are left in the dark. Without analysis an adverse profit variance of £15 is a matter for surmise; it might stem for example from the default of a debtor who owed this sum. Such an event would have just this effect on profit, and would need corrective action of a very different kind from the events we have been considering.

Corrective action presupposes an awareness of the causes of deviant behaviour. Human behaviour is complex, and nowhere more so than in the working situation. While variance analysis does not reveal why people in an organization do what they do, it does offer a quantified financial measure of the effect of their actions on financial progress. It thereby suggests some priorities in examining areas of the business where achievements are different from original intentions, and where plans and actions can be constructively modified.

Each of these variances has a message for somebody in the organization. In a larger business, one with more functional specialization than would be likely inside Industrial Units Ltd., it would be possible as a first step to allot the variances to different functions:

Sales variances: sales manager.

Materials price variance: purchasing officer.

Materials usage variance: factory supervision.

Labour rate variance: personnel manager.

Labour efficiency variance: factory supervision.

Variable overhead expenditure variance: factory supervision, maintenance engineer, purchasing officer, etc.

Fixed overhead capacity variance: personnel manager.

Fixed overhead efficiency variance: factory supervision.

Fixed overhead expenditure variance: administration manager.

The reason for allotting variances in this way is that different managers have different and specialized responsibilities for getting results and taking corrective action. A moment's thought will show that the simple allotment of variances shown above ignores the two-way influence which people in organizations usually have on each other, whether laterally or up and down in the "chain of command" as it is sometimes called. For example, the foreman may request the purchasing officer to buy higher grade and more expensive raw material because of the excessive scrap and wasted time emerging from the attempts of his men to process the cheaper material specified in the budget. The personnel manager, noting the high turnover of clerical staff, may suggest an overspending on supervisory training (not budgeted for) as a means of building up a more effective and less costly office organization, and reducing staff replacement costs.

The biggest reciprocal influence of all is, of course, that between production and sales. Sales variances are really deliveries variances, and the sales mix will often be heavily influenced by what the factory has been able to produce rather than by what orders the sales force has been able to get.

The system of variance reporting adopted should correspond with the commitment to objectives, i.e. the motivations to organizational goals, which result from the process of agreeing performance standards and setting targets. The usefulness of standard costs and budgets lies in the significance of the variances to which they give rise, and the significance of variances lies in the direction and strength of the motivation they produce. The effect of a knowledge of variances is to stimulate an examination of the actions which brought about the variances, and of the conditions in which these actions were taken. This leads to a comparison of the actions and conditions with those assumed in setting standards and drawing up budgets, and a judgement as to whether the actions taken were the most desirable in the situation actually encountered. From the financial point of view, desirability is judged against the particular balance between profitability and liquidity chosen for the budget period under review.

Two general points emerge from this description of variance analysis: first, that the process of control is continuous and circular, affecting everyone in the business who has a real job to do. A periodical variance summary for top management should not be the sole or even the main stimulus to corrective action. It is essentially a summary of the influence on profit of individual and group effort in the conditions actually prevailing during the control period. The second point is that variance analysis itself does not show why things turned out as they did. It indicates the areas where the influence on profit differed from expectations, and like ratio analysis raises questions which need answers.

The variance analysis carried out in the Industrial Units Ltd. illustration reveals a general picture not unknown in business: turnover up, production up, longer hours worked, but profit down. This analysis was based on full costing, and therefore focused attention on full standard cost and sales value. Contribution is a more positive focus for marketing people, since it measures the incremental revenue at stake in a given sales programme, rather than the order-book value. (From this point of view, salesman's commission based on turnover can be a most misleading incentive, particularly if product P/V ratios are significantly different.) We can quickly reshape the variance summary in contribution terms, beginning with the comparison shown in Table 80.

The change in contribution as between the original and adjusted budgets is shown above to be an increase of £19. This can be derived from the full costing budget of Table 76: contribution increase equals increase in standard profit (£11) plus over-recovery of fixed overhead (£8). The point is that under full costing it has to be derived. It is not clearly disclosed as the main variable and operationally controllable factor in profit achievement (assuming that fixed costs are determined by longer-term policy and are not expected to change much if at all during the immediate budget period).

The difference between the standard contribution in the adjusted budget (£124) and the actual contribution (£92) results partly from changes in the volume (i.e. quantity and mix) of activity, and partly from changes in the cash flows generated by

TABLE 80. INDUSTRIAL UNITS LTD.

Comparison of Standard Contribution Yield in Original and Adjusted Week 1 Budgets

	Type A		Type B		Type C		Total
Unit contribution (see Table 70)	£3		£2		£5		—
	Qty.	Contribution	Qty.	Contribution	Qty.	Contribution	Total contribution
		£		£		£	£
Original budget	20	60	10	20	5	25	105
Adjusted budget	16	48	18	36	8	40	124
Actual		Available in subsidiary schedules					92

each unit of activity (i.e. one unit of product produced and sold). The cash flow generated by activity is the cash inflow from customers and the cash outflow mainly to suppliers and production workers. (Cash costs of fixed overheads are largely the costs of preparing for activity rather than of the manufacturing and selling activity itself.) Contribution will thus approximate to the net cash generation calculated for specific capital projects. Taken together, these projects will represent the total activity of the business, assuming for the moment a business larger than Industrial Units Ltd. It was explained in Chapter 5 that cash flows for capital projects excluded all depreciation and apportioned fixed costs. It will frequently be the case, therefore, that the net result

TABLE 81. INDUSTRIAL UNITS LTD.

Variance Summary, Week 1, Based on Contribution Analysis

	£	£
Original budgeted contribution		105
Actual contribution		92
Total contribution variance		13 (A) ←
Variances due to changes in volume:		
Quantity	21 (F)	
Mix	2 (A)	
		19 (F)
Variances due to changes in unit prices and costs:		
Sales price	10 (A)	
Cost of materials:		
Price	7 (A)	
Usage	10 (A)	
Cost of labour:		
Rate	11 (A)	
Efficiency	6 (F)	
		32 (A)
Total contribution variance		13 (A) ←
Fixed overhead expenditure variance		2 (A)
Net profit variance		15 (A)
Original budgeted profit		55
Actual net profit		£40

of sales price variances and variable cost expenditure variances will provide a ready index of the way in which predicted net cash generations are being realized. It is no coincidence that certain firms which make good use of capital expenditure appraisal techniques are also very contribution conscious.

A management which adopts the marginal approach will find the variance summary of Table 81 of more use than the one in Table 79.

This summary is drawn up on the assumptions of break-even analysis, modified in the light of actual results. The assumption is first made that a percentage increase in quantity of output will bring a corresponding increase in contribution. Thus the original contribution of £105 is increased by 20% (£21) in accordance with the 20% increase in quantity of units from 35 to 42. The mix in

TABLE 82. INDUSTRIAL UNITS LTD.

Contribution Mix Variance: Week 1

Actual total quantity, budgeted mix:

Type	% mix	Quantity	Unit contribution	Total contribution
			£	£
A	57	24	3	72
B	29	12	2	24
C	14	6	5	30
Total	100	42		126

Actual total quantity, actual mix:

Type	% mix	Quantity	Unit contribution	Total contribution
			£	£
A	38	16	3	48
B	43	18	2	36
C	19	8	5	40
Total	100	42		124

products actually sold is not, however, the same as that budgeted, so a mix variance is calculated (Table 82).

The mix turns out to have only a small effect on contribution, but this might well be fortuitous. The reasons for the mix change need to be investigated: did customers request it, or did production staff adopt it to increase throughput?

The next stage in the analysis corresponds with the sales price variance calculation shown earlier in this chapter. But because contribution is "under attack" by both selling price and production cost, these two factors are isolated and separately analysed.

Finally, the fixed cost expenditure variance is taken into account. This leads to the same net profit variance as in the full costing analysis. The two sets of figures are saying basically the the same thing, but the emphasis is different.

The contribution-based variance summary discloses nothing about theoretically under-used capacity. As far as labour hours are concerned, it concentrates on the real situation: how did the pace of work compare with the standard pace? It is assumed that a shortfall in input hours will be dealt with in other ways.

Summary

Standard costs offer guidance to management in controlling the business cycle. The process of transforming current assets into debtors, cash, and profits requires vigilance and skill to prevent dissipation of financial resources.

Marketing staff are guided by their commitment to seek target sales goals, which can be expressed as either turnover or contribution. Contribution goals focus on the net incremental benefit expected by the company from a specific sales programme. Sales or contribution variances highlight the difference between planned achievement in this direction and actual achievement.

The second factor affecting contribution is variable cost. The main items of variable cost are direct materials, direct labour, and variable overhead. These are the factors of production directly controlled by factory supervision, who are guided in their use or release of these resources by predetermined limits on expense levels called standard costs. Cost variances measure the extent of progress up to or over the predetermined cost limits, which vary with the level of activity.

Fixed overheads, too, are predetermined, but by reference to policy decisions rather than to the level of activity. Fixed costs may be apportioned to units of product, as in full costing, or left in an aggregate amount to be deducted from contribution. Either way, the fixed overhead variances draw attention to the difference between planned and actual fixed costs.

All variances, whether of cost or revenue, have an effect on profit which can be analysed and broadly attributed to the different production, marketing, and administrative groups where financial decisions are made.

Standards and variances are the main financial tools for controlling the flow of costs through a business, the return flow of revenues, and the net income which is measured by matching the costs and revenues.

CHAPTER 9

A Note on Pricing

WE HAVE not yet considered the price-fixing decision itself. All that has been said on current asset circulation, sales revenue, and price–volume relationships has assumed a price, or has indicated the profit consequences if this or that price secured this or that volume of sales. Some discussion of the pricing decision itself is now called for, since marketing people will be called on to contribute to this decision and to live with it after it has been made.

The importance of the decision needs no stress. The price of a product is a statement of the extent to which the owners of a business, or their representatives, require to replenish and increase their purchasing power, in return for the surrender of their stock-in-trade or the performance of a service. For this reason, the pricing decision is generally reserved for top management, although in jobbing industries it will frequently need to be delegated. Furthermore, the seller has normally to make the decision before he enters the market, whether or not he communicates it.

Because price is the financial basis of exchange, the pricing decision can seldom be made without reference to other parties in the exchange. These other parties are found in the market: prospective buyers and competitors. Nowadays there is increasing intervention from a third source—the government, acting on behalf of what it sees to be the public interest. As usual in situations where there are interacting variables, the final decision will rest on an optimum balance between the interests of purchaser, seller, the trade generally (which brings in competitors), and society at large. This balance is the balance between supply and demand, and in a self-regulating market the level of demand is brought towards the level of supply by changes in price. Prices rise when demand is greater than supply; prices fall when supply is greater than demand. Any standard text on economics will explain and qualify the law of supply and demand more fully than is necessary here.

The first step in a pricing decision is therefore to consider the current state of demand. This means considering the buyer, i.e. the prospective customer. What is the present demand for products or services like ours? How much do customers pay for the product? How much will they pay if we increase the supply by a given number of units? It may be that there is a known market price for the product, that customers will not pay any more than this, and that there is no good reason why they should pay less. In this case, there is no pricing problem. Either you adopt the market price or you keep out of this particular market.

However, there is more to the problem than this, and we can usefully summarize the main influences which lead purchasers to behave as they do, on the assumption that they have sufficient purchasing power to enter the market. The main influences are: value of product to buyer, range of buyer choice, the presence of other buyers, and degree of buying skill.

The more valuable the product to the buyer, the more he will pay for it. But there are different kinds of value, and the distinction between use value and esteem value is particularly important. Use value arises when possession of the product enables the owner to change his way of doing things so that the new way is more beneficial to him than the old way. It was the main ploy of the traditional "hard seller" to impress on his prospective customer the use value of the product to him. A good example of use value is quoted by Peter Drucker.* He cites the case of an electrical engineering firm supplying

* Peter F. Drucker, *The Practice of Management*, Heinemann, 1955, chapter 6, in the section "What is value to the customer?"

fuse-boxes and switchboards to electrical contractors. This firm recognized that speed of installation was more important to the contractors than low price, because the contractors make their profit on materials rather than on labour. Consequently, they preferred a high material cost and a low labour cost. Apparently, it is traditional in the United States for electrical contractors to charge customers little more than their actual labour costs, but double the material costs. To the contractor, the cheapest and most valuable product is the one which gives the householder the lowest contract price, and gives himself the lowest installation cost by the highest margin on materials. "And if price is value", says Drucker, "then high manufacturer's price is better value for the electrical contractor."

Esteem value also motivates buyers. Esteem value arises when possession of the product appears to the owner to raise his status above the status of those who do not possess the product. This sort of value is not limited to luxury goods like Jaguar sports cars or exclusive gowns. Even computer manufacturers have cashed in on it. The higher the status conferred, the more will the buyer pay. When ball-point pens first came out around 1946, people paid pounds rather than shillings for the early models, and there was clearly an element of esteem value in having one. Certainly the use value of the first ball-point pens was considerably lower than that of current models costing only a few pence, which last longer and smudge less than the early ones.

The notion of value for money underlies the fascination of a bargain. The alternative to stressing superior value is to stress lower price for the same value. The lower price is usually temporary, and this also has the paradoxical effect of allaying buyer suspicion that a permanently lower price may mean lower quality.

The next influence was range of buyer choice, and this involves a look at competitors. Competition is, however, a matter of fact. A firm in the same line of business may or may not be a competitor in a given market at a particular time. Indeed, there are often explicit agreements among firms not to compete. It is important, in arriving at a price decision, to ask, "Who else is offering a price, and what prices are they offering, or likely to offer?" Construction firms have to do most of their pricing on this basis, with one eye on costs: the cost if the job is obtained, and the cost if it is not. The need to recognize the price levels of competitors has already been touched on, but in the context of giving use or esteem value for money, we can modify the limitations imposed by the notion of a single acceptable market price. The question becomes "How does the use or esteem value conferred on the customer by my product compare with the use or esteem value to him of competing products?" If customers find it hard to see the additional use value you claim for your product, then the chances are that it has none, and attempts to get away with a higher price will be unlikely to succeed.

Buyer choice covers not only similar products from different suppliers, but different products with similar uses. It is a well known dictum in buying circles that you do not buy a product, you buy a function. Consequently beef competes with lamb, telephones compete with mail, adhesives compete with screws. This is the well-known economic factor of substitution, which is at the root of all problems of resource utilization and economic exchange. Because commodities, particularly raw or semi-processed commodities, have a variety of uses, and because needs can be satisfied in a variety of ways, economic life is an endless process of choice among alternatives or substitutes. The acceptable price of a commodity will therefore be somewhere near the price of its substitutes.

The freedom of a buyer to choose how he spends his money is also affected by the availability of complementary products, i.e. products bought and used in association with each other. Petrol and cars, or coal and coal-scuttles, are familiar examples. Changes in demand for one produce a corresponding change in demand for the other, and price movements of one will therefore produce corresponding price movements of the other. These assumptions all rest on the existence of a free market, in which prices result from the influence of supply and demand. Often enough, prices are government-influenced (through purchase-tax) so that supply and demand result from the influence of prices.

Another factor affecting the price which buyers will pay is the presence or absence of other buyers. An auction is a vivid illustration of the effect buyers have on each other. Every seller who hopes to remain an independent business would prefer to have many buyers. If there is only one buyer (economists call this "monopsony"), the seller is at his mercy and must accept that the buyer will have a major say in fixing the price. Recent hard bargaining between the Gas Council and the North Sea gas prospectors is a good example of this. More usually there are many buyers, and they will not normally expect to pay different prices for identical supplies (identical, that is, in specification and quantity). Apart from auctions, take-over bids, and black markets, buyers will not for long try to outbid each other for limited supplies. Price maintenance by restriction of supply will eventually bounce back on the seller, for buyers will seek alternatives, and perhaps leave the supplier high and dry.

The fourth factor we noticed was buying skill. Buying skill is found in the shrewd housewife and in the trained industrial or commercial buyer. On the whole, a seller can expect to find less impulse buying in industry than among consumers, but there is undoubtedly a good deal of prestige buying in industry, based more on desire to possess than need to use. Buying skill can certainly play a large part in determining the price level at which a deal is made, but this will generally happen only in situations where technical negotiation is possible. The very possibility of negotiation takes much of the problem out of pricing; the difficult decisions are those which have to be made unilaterally by the seller, without knowledge of similar unilateral decisions being made by competitors. A high degree of buying skill inside the inquiring firm may cause the seller to offer a lower price; a low degree of buying skill might tempt him to "try on" a high price. Marks & Spencers are well known for the care with which they buy; this certainly gives them a major say in the prices they will accept.

There is a great deal more to be said about buyer psychology and markets generally, but the above summarizes as much of the subject as is thought useful within the scope of this book. Notice that we took market readiness to pay as our first basis for pricing decisions. This is the view taken by economists, and it differs from the view usually put forward by accountants, namely that the price offered should give the supplier a fair or satisfactory margin of profit above his costs. This view now calls for comment.

It seems to be generally thought that firms base their prices on manufacturing or purchasing costs, plus a percentage mark-up to cover overheads and profit. The price thus arrived at can be modified a little according to the market situation. The percentage mark-up chosen will reflect financial and marketing policy within the firm and trade practice outside it. It is certain that most firms base their estimating and quoting activity on cost records. How else can you be sure of making a profit?

Studies by economists seem to show that this "cost-plus" mentality is not so widespread after all. Profit margins are highly variable, are not always closely related to changes in costs, are frequently "squeezed" by market pressures and sometimes expanded by price increases designed to increase profits rather than maintain the cost/profit ratio. "The whole feel of practical affairs is that prices are not, in fact, determined by firms solely on the basis of costs. Both supply and demand play their part."* The frequency with which one hears the phrase, "This product is made to a price", also belies the cost-plus attitude.

Reference to costs seems then to be more of a check on likely profitability than an arithmetical basis for firm price offers. As such it is worth while provided the precision of unit costs is not pushed too far, particularly unit total costs.

How far then can a look at costs help in trying to decide what price to charge? The answer seems to lie again in the marginal approach, which combines the economists' and the accountants'

* Bates, James, and Parkinson, J. R., *Business Economics*, Blackwell, Oxford, 1963.

viewpoints. Unit direct costs will give a good idea of the out-of-pocket costs likely to be incurred in fulfilling the order. Anything above this is contribution to fixed overheads. Total contribution, period by period, must exceed fixed costs, or there will be losses to report. The profit–volume chart of Fig. 9 (p. 166) together with an attempt to forecast likely demand at different prices, will be of great help in reconciling unit prices and periodic net profit requirements.

The extent to which contribution should exceed fixed costs depends on the company's need for profit. A company needs profits in order to survive and grow. To do this it must renew worn out assets, secure finance for expansion, and pay shareholders for the use of their money and the risks attaching to their investment.

Most accountants will recoil from this out-and-out advocacy of contribution pricing. They see its dangers all too clearly: give a marketing man only the direct or marginal cost on which to base his price, and he will sell below total cost all the time just to get orders.

Nobody who understands business could possibly advocate this. Contribution targets need to be set very carefully, and there can be no question of net profit until break-even point has been passed. But as the previous chapters argued, an intelligent search for contribution rather than turnover or unit net profit seems to be the best way for marketing people to help in optimizing profits.

The marginal approach also makes it fairly easy to measure the value added by the company to the raw materials and services it buys. The added value equals the sales value less the cost of bought out materials, components, and services. These bought out items represent the physical resources which the company, by skilful planning, organizing, and control, transforms into a product of greater value to customers, a value measured by the price agreed. The skill of management lies largely in creating as high a value as possible in the eyes of prospective customers, while consuming as little of this value as possible in fixed assets, wages, and salaries. The residue of unconsumed value is net profit; the creation of value and the effective utilization of resources is the essence of marketing and financial control.

Summary

This chapter can best be summarized by means of a check list of questions intended to help in fixing a price for a new product not yet on the market. The need for internal consistency in the firm's price list has therefore been ignored.

1. What is the present and likely future demand, if any, for competing products or services (whether competing directly or as substitutes and including our own products)? Is this demand linked to complementary products?
2. How much are customers paying for these competing products? What would the demand be at higher or lower prices?
3. What effect will the additional supply (from our new product) have on prices in this market?
4. How does the use, or esteem value, of the new product compare with that of competing products? Will use of our product genuinely save the customer money? How much? By how much will it increase his profit-earning capacity (industrial products)? Will it move his standard of living in the direction he desires (consumer products)?
5. How much additional price is appropriate to the additional customer benefit?
6. How many likely buyers are there? Do they all know how much other buyers are paying? How far do they see themselves as a market?
7. Is the new product to be offered in one market only or are there several markets? What price differences are appropriate or desirable in respect of each market?
8. What will it cost to produce and sell the product in different quantities? What will be the fixed, variable and total costs at different levels of production and sale?
9. What contribution will the product make at different prices and volumes?

10. How will sales of the product affect the total net profits of the business at different prices and volumes?
11. How low can the price be dropped and still provide (a) a worthwhile return on investment, or (b) worthwhile customer goodwill, or (c) work, for an organization which might otherwise have to be disbanded?
12. How high can the price be raised without loss of goodwill, and without attracting unwanted notice from competitors and government agencies?

Answers to these questions should not be dreamed up in an armchair. They should be sought wherever the information is—with the customer, within trade associations, in government directives, in short, with every source of market influence.

CHAPTER 10

Financial Information for Marketing Control

CHAPTERS 1–9 of this book have given a lot of financial information. It has been given in a way which will, it is hoped, be useful to people whose business life lies in marketing. Not all the information given in this book is relevant to every marketing job or situation, and our final problem is to select some criteria on which we can build and modify financial control systems. These criteria will be basic, and therefore applicable to business situations generally. The reader who is working inside the marketing function, and who is therefore helping to control it, will need to apply these criteria to his own job and to jobs he might do in the future.

The nature of a control system was described in Chapter 1, where we noted the simple fact that what makes things happen the way we want them to happen is a shared understanding with our fellow workers on what needs to happen. (This is stretching the word "happen" beyond its normal meaning; nothing happens of itself, everything has a cause.) Before we act, we must decide how to act; before we can decide, we must have information on the likely results of alternative actions. The two essential steps in control are therefore information and action: information on what needs to be brought about (the objective) and on what has already been brought about (progress); and action to modify progress or adjust objectives where they are out of line.

Problems of planning and control inside a business organization are always concerned with the interaction of human beings at work. What evidence there is on human interaction suggests that, given the necessary information and support, most people can direct themselves towards organizational goals, and do not need to be directed in the conventional way. The conventional way of getting results is simply for the manager to tell his staff what to do and to see that they do it. An alternative way is for the manager to arouse the interest of staff by sharing his problems with them, arriving with them at a common understanding of objectives, and helping them to set themselves progress targets. Many managers will see this as abdication, but there is plenty of evidence (a) that imposed decisions are resisted simply because they are imposed and regardless of their inherent merits, and (b) that many decisions are felt to be imposed and are therefore resisted regardless of whether or not the manager explicitly intends to impose them.*

The importance of this in the control process is that people in business organizations should have the information that they need to control themselves; they are unlikely to derive worth-while benefit either for themselves or for their organizations, by collecting a lot of routine information on the performance of others, particularly subordinates. Chapter 8 on standards and variances hinted at the joint target-setting approach which seems to be unusually promising as a means of improving business results.

In the financial sphere there are particular difficulties. Company balance sheet and profit and loss account information is generally thought to be highly confidential. Indeed, some managements go to extreme lengths to keep standard cost information off the shop floor, presumably for fear that unions or industrial spies will glean from it something that can be used to the company's disadvantage. This view is consistent with conventional approaches to managerial control. It is also thought that shop-floor

* For an extended treatment of managerial attitudes to influence and control, see Douglas McGregor, *The Human Side of Enterprise*, McGraw-Hill, New York, 1960. The whole book is a critique of traditional ways of interpersonal influence in industrial management.

workers cannot understand financial complexities. There are, however, many instances of numerical dexterity among manual workers. For example, worker ingenuity in mastering the complexities of piecework payment systems is well known. Sometimes considerable skill in manipulating output records is developed. Usually the aim is not to defraud the company but to satisfy a need for income stability, a need not always understood by management.

The main requirement of an effective information system will therefore be that it should provide each member of the organization with the information he needs to understand his aims and check his progress. The main problem is one of sorting out the relevant information from the irrelevant (when there is too much information) or of seeing clearly the relevant information which is lacking (when there is too little).

What makes financial information relevant? Generally speaking, information is relevant, and therefore useful, when it tells you:

> What financial results you should achieve.
> What progress you are making.
> What need and scope there is for corrective action.

Relevance assumes, of course, that the information is objectively verifiable and is reasonably undistorted. The more people who handle the information before it is acted on, the more distorted it is likely to become. Relevant information should also be obtainable at a cost proportionate to the benefits of using it. Within these limits it should be available when needed and be as up to date as possible.

We can distinguish between routine financial information needed regularly and special financial information needed to solve a non-recurring problem—big or small. The problem-solving information will often pave the way for further routine information, needed (perhaps for only a limited period of time) to check the effectiveness of the course of action adopted.

Regular information needs can often be clarified by asking such questions as:

What is my job, and what financial results am I expected to achieve (costs, revenues, profits, asset utilization)?

What could go wrong in achieving these results?

How, and how soon, can I find out if things are going wrong?

What corrective action can I take?

What corrective action do I expect other people to take?

What information do they need? What part if any have I to play in supplying information needed by others?

Special information needs are related to problem solving and decision making. The essence of financial problems is that there is some obstacle to the achievement of financial results and a number of alternative ways of overcoming the obstacle. Previous chapters have illustrated many such problems in the marketing area: Which products do we push? Which do we drop? Which project do we invest in? How can we expand sales without running an overdraft? Are selling expenses too high? Is this customer a good credit risk? How low can we drop our price?

Problem solving and decision making fill the day of most business managers. Before we discuss an approach to financial problems, two basic things need to be said; firstly, be sure that you have located the real problem, and, secondly, discuss problems with others involved—especially if they are subordinates. But recognize that getting the right people to involve themselves in a problem, or even to admit that a problem exists, can be a major problem in itself.

Here, then, are some points to watch for in attempting to solve business problems with a bearing on financial results (and there are few business problems without financial implications):

Concentrate on future cash flows

We can only control future actions; past expenditure is irretrievably committed, and cannot be changed by decisions taken now. This means that depreciation charges, which arise because of previous expenditure on fixed assets, are irrelevant to cost comparisons of alternative proposals. So are any other amounts by which unexpired costs are written down. Previous expenditures, sometimes called "sunk costs", can therefore be ignored. Apportioned costs, too, are frequently unaffected by decisions affecting the section or unit to which they are apportioned, and such costs should be excluded from cost comparisons of alternatives if they will not be affected in total. This leaves us with "cash costs", and in practice the information we need to solve a problem will be the effect of the decision on future receipts and payments of cash, i.e. future cash flows.

Concentrate on the relevance and size of the amounts

Whether the amounts involved are precisely known or whether they are only approximations matters less than their relevance (to the cash flow) and size in relation to the total cash gain at stake in the problem. This in turn should be related to total turnover, net profit and contribution during the period of time to which the decision applies.

Recognize the strength of the reasons for each alternative

Recognize the strength rather than the total number of reasons listed for or against the proposals. One argument for a proposal may be strong enough to override ten arguments against it.

State the assumptions

Information can never be complete, and there will always be gaps. We plug these gaps with assumptions. Every prediction rests on assumptions, many of which can be quantified, and these assumptions should be stated clearly, if only to invite other people's help in correcting them. This is particularly necessary in framing budgets.

Recognize margins of error

These can often be calculated by statistical formulae. If the degree of error or uncertainty is difficult to quantify, try a best, worst and most likely estimate of the financial outcome.

Make a positive decision

Delaying a decision has the same effect as confirming the present arrangements, and this may or may not be desirable.

Recognize that emotions influence people's actions as much as reasoning

If we are in favour of a certain course of action, we shall tend to minimize the costs of doing it; if we are against it, we shall pile up costs against it. Enthusiasm, logical argument, and an abundance of detailed financial information in support of the proposal bring no guarantee that others will agree with it.

Financial information, important though it is, is only part of the story

A good note on which to end this book. There are many aspects of business life and problems which the accounting function by its very nature cannot measure. While financial information and understanding is a necessary aid to marketing analysis and business decisions, it is not a sufficient aid; nor is it a substitute for professional competence, managerial judgement, and the skills whereby human beings influence each others' behaviour.

Index